Confessions of a Lady Pilot

Dear Tricia

I love heels + goggles.

Here Skier

Amanda x

Copyright © Amanda Harrison Confessions Of A Lady Pilot 2013

ALL RIGHTS RESERVED.

No part of this book may be reproduced in any form whatsoever, electronic, or mechanical, including photocopying, recording, or by any informational storage or retrieval system without the expressed written authority, dated and signed permission from the author Amanda Harrison.

ALL INTELLECTUAL PROPERTY RIGHTS SUBSISTING IN THE DESIGN OR CONTENT OF THIS BOOK ARE THE PROPERTY OF AMANDA HARRISON,

This First Edition Published by,

Tawny Owl Publishing of

PO BOX 392 Carterton OX18 9DS.

This book is dedicated to my dearest Mum and Dad,
without them none of this would have been possible.
They have always given me love and support
no matter what crazy idea I have.
Including the crazy idea that I can fly!

Contents

Yes I am A Woman	6
Chocks Away!	17
My Thighs Have Control	26
The View Out Of the Office Window	35
The Original Tiger Moth Pilots	41
Taming The Tiger Moth	44
The Naked Pilot	48
The Fashion Police	51
A Bank Robber Pilot	57
Pilot For Hire Anyone?	63
Anyone Can Do It If I Can	71
Achieving The Im-'Possible' Dreams	76
What A Weird Way To Make A Living, People Trying To Kill You Every Day	81
All The Gear And No Idea	87
Tail Dragger Pilots , Make The Best Lovers	93
Falling In Love With The Tiger Moth	99
Why Do We Fly? Icarus, Freedom, Empowerment, View, Challenge, To Feel Like An Explorer, All Of The Above	108
The Real Glamour Of Flying	112
Never Fitted In Until Now My Home Is In The Sky	116

Yes I Am A Woman

And Yes I Really Am Your Pilot

Murder: that is what I am thinking. Just take them round the back and hit them over the head with the fire extinguisher – the correct kind of fire extinguisher, of course, the foam one. I mean, I am a trained professional, so the correct procedures would have to be carried out, of course. I loved doing my fire and safety course. It was absolutely fantastic learning how to drag unconscious people out of aeroplanes and, of course, the golden rule is never make yourself a casualty so sometimes you just have to save yourself. However, I digress.

It is one of those days where I wish I could just fast-forward to the end of the flight where they are kissing me and hugging me and a little bit over-exuberant and telling me what a wonderful experience they have just had and how much they enjoyed it and how they are not scared at all now. However, for the first flight of the day, it is always a little bit difficult and I suppose it is the whole crux of the matter – and why I am confessing to you about lady pilots, is that I am completely not what the customers and passengers expect.

They walk out to their flight experience and they imagine that they are going to be met with a Second World War fighter pilot ace who's a little bit grizzled, greying hair, moustache, six feet tall, slightly rugged, good-looking and with the attitude of slightly bored by all this flying now. And what do they get? They get me – a younger version of that and a lady. "Full marks for your observation," I want to say sometimes. Gee, I had not noticed that I am a woman, female of the species. I can understand that the aeroplane and I sort of go against the conventional rules of what you expect when you walk out to fly a Tiger Moth.

I mean, this is a typical flying day with the Tiger Moth. On this day, what I do is I take people up for their air experience flights. So they have bought – either on the internet or through the airfield – an experience of being taken up in a classic, vintage aeroplane, open cockpit, for the experience of their lives flying as the World War II pilots used to. And they come up, expecting it to be perfect, being able to fly on any kind of day, any kind of weather, no matter what the weather and have this fantastic experience with this grizzled old Spitfire pilot. It is one of my many jobs and it is a job that I love because, on a good day when the weather is playing and the aeroplane is playing and both of them are behaving themselves, it means I get to fly people in the sky in the lovely aeroplane – one of my most favourite aeroplanes, the Tiger Moth, a vintage, open cockpit aeroplane – and introduce people to the reasons why I love flying. In fact, all the time they come back with what we call the "Tiger grin on their face," having loved the experience and having really enjoyed it. The first problem is – and this is the whole point of why I sort of snapped the hand off the person who offered me this job – is I truly am flying or living my dream. I fly the aeroplane that I love on days that are great and take people up and show them the magic of flying. It really is living the dream and how many people really get to do that? How many people really get to achieve some of their real deep-in-their heart achievements?

The trouble is it is not quite as glamorous as you would think. On a typical Tiger Moth flying day, after we have pushed the aeroplane out of the hangar, I check it over, as a conscientious pilot always does and end up covered in oil, out of breath and slightly sweating, not a very glamorous part of the flying experience.. In fact – and I often say this to people – in the Highway Code, it says you should check your car out every time before you get in the car. And I ask people this if they are winding me up. I say, "Tell me what is wrong with your car. Tell me what you should do with your car before you get in the aeroplane." When we go through all the safety things, if they are getting sort of upset that we have to give them a safety brief, I point out to them that it is most difficult to get out of an aeroplane. You cannot just land on a cloud and get out and sort whatever the technical problem, or the problem with the passenger, is. So we have to do all the briefing for safety and for technical reasons on the ground. And, the Highway Code states, for your car, "You should check your tyres and all your fluid levels including water for the car," not for the windscreen wash, but you should check that as well, "and also your oil level." And you are supposed to check that all your lights are working. How many people can remember that? Because if you get stopped – here is a tip for you – if you get stopped by the police and they say, "One of your lights is out," then you say, "Oh, really? Oh, that must have just gone." This really is a confessional?

Now, I have never been stopped for that, for my lights, by the way; I just want to clarify that. But you should check your car before you get into it. And as pilots, we are taught to check our aeroplanes before we get into them. If we find any problems, we do not go. We get into different aeroplanes because, as I say, it is very difficult to land on a cloud and step out onto it to check your aeroplane. The aeroplane's quite happy landing on the cloud; it is when you step out onto it that you tend to see that you are not quite an angel yet and your own wings have not actually grown. So, while I am getting checked out, I try to do it very diligently and nicely, but these old aeroplanes – and any aeroplane actually – tend to give you a little bit of a kick in the morning so as you are checking the oil, that will spurt all over you and get all over your fingers. As you check the fuel that normally mixes in with the oil, it makes a nice hand cream to make your hands nice and smooth. Then there are other things; for instance, you will want to get rid of all the dead flies if you have not gotten rid of them the previous day, so you get a bit of blood and guts mixed in with that nice hand cream. So you tend to smell a bit like oil, Avgas, and Jet A1 depending on which aeroplane you are flying and you do get normally quite splattered with the aforesaid liquids. There are other problems as well. You have to make sure that the sick bag – although I refer to it as the tip bag (more of that later) – is in place and not got any holes in it. So, even before you have got to the customer, you are beginning to smell a little bit like the aeroplane itself, which, actually, I do not mind. I quite like the smell of aviation fuel, but then again I am probably a bit weird. In fact, I will certify that. I am very weird.

The next problem is getting the person over the fact I am a woman. Actually, when they walk into our little briefing room and I bound over to them and say, "Yes, I am your pilot for today," the look on their faces often is priceless. The polite people just sort of hold out their hands and cough a little and say, "Oh, very nice to meet you," while they are really thinking, *Oh, dear lord, it is a woman pilot. This is not what I expected. Now I am scared.* The secondary, sort of middle polite people, when I bound over and say, "Hi, I am your pilot for today," may actually turn around and say, "Oh, you are err, em, err, em," and then I will go, "Yes, I am a woman. Full marks for observation. You are going to get on well in the aeroplane." And then they get a bit embarrassed and say, "No, no, no, I did not mean that; it is quite all right. But how long have you been flying for?" And, depending on the time of the day if this is the first customer, I say, "Well, I have not actually flown anything today." I know, it is an old joke and it is getting very tired. A bit like the Tiger Moth, really. But their questions are how long have I flown for? And at the time of writing this, it is 14 years; since I started my Private Pilots License.

And how long have I been flying the Tiger? At the time of writing this, I have been commercially flying Tigers for four years. I have been flying Tigers longer than that, but commercially I have been flying them for four years. But that is what I normally reply to them. And I wish I could have that stamped on my forehead so that they could just read it. Maybe we will print that on the actual voucher thing, saying, "Here is how long I have flown for." However it is interesting that, in diving, they do teach you to check your instructor's qualifications. I am fine about that. I am perfectly happy for anybody to look at my license and check my qualifications, and in some ways, in the aviation world, we are the only people that do not have all our certificates up on the wall. Sometimes you go into a flying club and you will find that the certificates of safety and the certificates of the fire crew are up on the wall for the actual airfield, but seldom, almost never are there certificates up there to say that the pilots are trained and that the aircraft are actually certifiable to go and have been maintained correctly. All the paperwork is kept in books, and as pilots, we have our own licenses. However, I can understand why people ask the question. And maybe it is vanity as well; maybe I look so young that they do not think that I could have been flying a Tiger for that long. Thank you very much to the people that think that.

Then you get the bottom sort of class of politeness, where they just come straight out with it as you bound over and say, "Hi, I am your pilot today." They just say, "Good grief, you are a woman." To which I reply, "No, surely not? I must have changed in the night." So, I always try to make a bit of a joke of it because if I turn around and get offended we would not start off right. But I do get in my confessional note; it does get a bit wearing that it is every single time. And it is quite funny that often it is the wives of the male customers who get even more upset. I did actually have one woman threaten to sue me if I did not bring her husband back. I was not quite sure what to say to that, so I just walked out to the aeroplane, got in and flew, and he came back and had the biggest smile on his face ever. And she actually came out and gave me a kiss afterwards. But I did think about saying, "Well, hang on a minute. I will sue you for libel for just saying that." No. It is very, very funny the reactions of people when they see me because I realise that I am maybe totally the opposite of what they are expecting in their minds. This is a great shame because if you go back to when the Tiger Moths were originally flown in the 1930s and the 1940s, a lot of them were flown, positioned by women Pilots. The Air Transport Auxiliary (ATA) had a lot of lady pilots, so it is such a shame that this hasn't been promoted more.

The next thing we give them is the safety brief and they are now fully terrified, which is great. I like the customers to be slightly terrified and slightly scared and the reason is that they will listen more to the safety briefing and they will listen more in the air to what you are saying. It is people that actually come along and are cocky and sort of like, "Yes, I am funny," and do not tell you that they are nervous, they are the ones you have got to watch because they are the ones that are not actually listening to the safety brief and are not actually listening to you telling them how to fly the aeroplane. So, we have given them the safety brief, they are nicely scared, and now we walk out to the aeroplane and we take a load of photos with them – this is when I hide in the office doing the paperwork because I have had so many photos of my backside in the aeroplanes I hide round the corner so that they can take the glory. I have the best ground crew in the world. They are absolutely fantastic. Without them I would not be able to do the job. Rita takes the customers out and shows them how to stand looking like, "This is my aeroplane and I own this aeroplane."

So, we take them out, get the pictures done and then the fun starts of getting in and out of the Tiger Moth. Okay, so let me explain this to you. It is kind of half a horse and half a motorcycle and all of an aeroplane. What you have to do is you have to stand on the wing, which sounds scary in itself, but there is a designated step point. Then you have to hoist your leg over, most unladylike, into the cockpit and stand on the seat. This is one of the reasons why we do not tend to fly in the rain because your backside gets covered in mud. Once you have accomplished getting both feet inside the cockpit you, then have to lower yourself down, with your legs either side of the control column or stick. To me, this is a laugh a minute because most people do not have any upper body strength, so the way that they sit down in the aeroplane is very funny. A lot of people will start to go down, their knees will sag, their arms will give in and – *boof!* – they will sit down like a ton of bricks.

So, the getting in and out of the aeroplane of the Tiger Moth itself is quite difficult and always gives me a bit of a giggle when I watch people trying to get in and out. Again, we give them very explicit instructions on how to get in and out and we help them and this is where, as I say, my ground crew are fabulous. Rita is brilliant at placing her hands on various parts of people's anatomy without it actually being anything sexual or any kind of the wrong kind of place because, as you will imagine, trying to help somebody physically in and out or onto a horse, a motorbike, or into an aeroplane means that you do have to sometimes put your hands on various parts of their body. Most of the time, it is easier to lift them up by their underarms and their elbows and sort of push them up that way. Or, we place a hand on their backs to sort of help push them forward or lower them back when they are getting out. Depending on what they do, that hand ends up on their backsides and you are thinking, *No, that was not where I wanted my hand at all,* especially when they are nervous before they get into the aeroplane. And of course, the other problem is that we get the customer in first and then as I am getting in the aeroplane, you know that the rest of the family and friends are taking lots and lots of pictures, so as I am swinging my leg over horse-style to get into the aeroplane, does my bum look big in this photo? Absolutely. All the time.

Chocks Away!

Let me explain to you: the Tiger Moth is a bi-plane, which means it has got two sets of wings and then a slim fuselage with tandem seating. We sit the customer in the front and I sit behind; there are dual controls so that I can stop anything that they are doing wrong, basically. The engine in front is a Gipsy Major engine. It is a four-cylinder upside down engine. So, in your car, your engine sits upright and the spark plugs and all the oil and fuel and everything gets thrown in at the top. For some mad reason, the designers of this particular aeroplane decided that it would be best suited if they put the engine in upside down. I think the reasons were so they could put the propeller on the end of the crankshaft. Have I lost a few people yet? Probably, but do not worry. Basically, what it means is that the oil and the fuel and everything collects in the bottom of the cylinders and creates all sorts of problems in the Tiger Moth.

The starting of this kind of aeroplane? It is none of this airliner business, where the pilots get in and it says 'press this button to start' and they just press it and the engines wind up and they chuck the fuel in and away it goes. No, no, no. So, if the customers in the front weren't scared enough, now that they have got me flying them in the back, then they are going to be even more scared by the starting procedure of this aeroplane. And unless you have seen it before – unless you understand the world of vintage aeroplanes – you are going to think that this is very scary. Alan, the ground person, has to go to the front and place his fingers on the propeller and turn it around, almost like he was starting a windmill. He pulls his hand down briskly and then walks away very fast because if the aeroplane starts, it is going to go straight forward and possibly chew him up, and that can just get all messy. I mean, blood on grass just makes a mess.

So, we put what we call chocks under the wheels because the Tiger Moth does not have any brakes. Are you getting scared yet? So, with the chocks firmly in front of the tyres, we can go though the start procedure which is: Al will put in fuel into the engine using a little button on the side of the engine. The customer sees the bonnet being opened and a little button being pressed and sometimes also we have to hammer it. Then, he closes the bonnet and walks round the front of the aeroplane, we both switch some switches on the side of the cockpit and then we start shouting at one another. The reason we shout at one another is actually quite boring: it is because I have got my headset on and Al's at the front and if other aeroplanes are around on the airfield, then we want to shout – we want to make a definite noise to know exactly what is going on. Because, believe it or not, the ground crew at this point actually has control: what we call control of the aeroplane. Al is controlling what happens with the aeroplane because he is the person who's going to get bitten if it all goes wrong. So, he then says, "Contact," and I then yell back, "Contact," which is what you have heard in the films – quite cool, really –and he then winds the propeller round for the first go. Sometimes it bursts into life – *Rah*! A big cheer and away we go. More often than not, the aeroplane says, "No, you think you are going to fly today? No, you have not paid me enough attention; you have not polished me enough. I wanted an oil change and you still have not given me an oil change…" and I can see the aeroplane looking at me, going, "Yes, I am going to make your life miserable today." So, after about 10 winds of the propeller, I turn the switches off and go back and pour more fuel in and then Al winds the propeller backwards and then we start shouting again, "Contact!" Sometimes it can take a few goes to start the aeroplane. So, if the customers weren't scared before they got in, they are now really scared because I am not talking to them a lot because I am concentrating on my ground crew, which is what I should be doing. Sometimes I tell the customer what is going on but a lot of the time I cannot tell the customer what is going on because I am concentrating on the ground crew. So they are really scared now because it has taken more than one swing to start this aeroplane and they are thinking, *I want to get out now. Please let me go. I do not want to go in this aeroplane.*

The first thing that I say, as soon as I switch the radios on between me and the customer is, "Do not worry. Now that we have got her started, she will be fine." And the thing is, these days, when you jump into your car, you turn the key and it starts, 99 times out of 100. What used to happen with older cars is you used to have a mixture lever. I can remember one car that had this. The mixture lever was something that you had to slowly push in and if you got the consistency or the amount of mixture wrong, you would have what was called "flooding the engine" with too much fuel so it would start with a bang. Other times, you would not give it enough fuel. So, back then, you had a little mixture thing whereas now cars are very intelligent and work it all out for themselves. And so do modern aeroplanes. Modern aeroplanes do all this for us as well; we just get in and press the button or turn the key and it goes. However, this is the fun of flying a vintage aeroplane. Did I say fun?

So now that we have got started, we call on the radio and the radio calls on the ground are quite good. So we call, "Tiger Moth, radio check and airfield information." At this point, we have the video switched on as well; we are being videoed in the air, so I try and tell the customer, "No swearing as we take off." On the ground, we can normally speak to one another; it is when we get in the air that the problem comes. So, we taxi out and I am beginning to feel sorry for the customer now. The customer is seated in the front, and as we are taxiing out, after I have said the very famous words of, "Chocks away!", which is actually a signal because nobody can hear you saying chocks away but do not tell anybody that because the customers love to shout "chocks away!" So we shout "chocks away!" and we signal to the ground crew. The ground crew then takes the chocks away and off we go.

As we taxi down, there is another thing that scares the customers. The Tiger Moth is what you call a "tail dragger", so its tail on the ground, it drags its tail along the ground while it is on the ground. Once in the air, it picks it up by about two feet so it flies level. But on the ground, with the nose in the air, I am sitting in the back cockpit, they are sitting in the front and no one can see anything in front of them. You are beginning to think that the design of this aeroplane was not really good. I agree. The trouble is, in the olden days, when this aeroplane was first built and first used in earnest, there were massive round fields with lots and lots and lots of ground crew, not just two. There used to be about ten ground crew per aeroplane and the crew used to physically push the aeroplane into the wind and just take off. And when it landed, it also landed into wind and then the ground crew would rush out and walk, with one person either side of the wing, back to where the plane had started. This meant that the pilots did not normally have to do a lot of taxiing by themselves and fending for themselves; whereas, these days, we now have these bothersome things called "designated runways", where we have to land pointing in the direction of the runway. This is really a bit awkward when we are in a Tiger Moth because a Tiger Moth just likes to take off and land into wind. It'd be helpful if it could just land sideways on a runway, but for legal and safe reasons, we cannot always do that. So I have to taxi down to wherever the runway start is and while we are taxiing down, as I say, I cannot see anything in front of our nose, so I am scaring the passenger to death because I weave from side-to-side as though I have had far too many gin and tonics the night before (or the morning) and as we taxi. I stick my head out to have a look at what is in front of us, and then weave the other way, stick my head out again and have another look at what is in front of us. I do this in case there are things on the grass airfields like rabbits, or a dog might run in front of us; there could be anything, like all sorts of bags or anything left behind by other people. There is a footpath, so I have got to check that people are not going in front of that and I need to steer our way out of the path of other aeroplanes.

The problem is that, these days, because most aeroplanes have brakes and as I said the Tiger Moth does not, I have to stop by just using the inertia or losing the inertia – which pilots on other aeroplanes, if they have not been in a Tiger or a vintage aeroplane of this type, do not understand. So they will rush towards us, off the runway, or taxi next to us, thinking that we can stop and let them by, or thinking that we can go side-by-side quite easily. So sometimes I get an aeroplane that rushes off the runway in front of me and I have to stop and wave it by and say, "I have not got any brakes, I am sorry. You are asking me to manoeuvre in too small an area I mean ..." Come on I am a woman! I need a bigger place to manoeuvre and park, you know. Give me a chance.

So, we are trundling down the runway and then I give the customer the brief and I say, "It will all get quite loud and noisy and blowy with the slipstream, of course, being an open air cockpit, so I won't talk to you while we are doing the take-off run. I will just let you enjoy the actual experience. It is all going to get rather loud and noisy now. Are you ready?" Sometimes the customers say yes. No, I lie. I always wait until they say yes. By that time, they are strapped in and they think, *Well, I am going to die anyway so I may as well die in the air*. I can tell the people that are thinking that. So, we turn onto the runway, I tell them over the radio that Tiger Moth is rolling and away we go. This is where my dream starts. All of that messing around, sorting the aeroplane, all of that – checking it, getting the customers, safety brief, all of that 'Yes, you are a woman pilot, what a surprise' – all of that disappears as I smoothly open the throttle and apply the control stick forward to pick the tail up as we trundle down the runway.

I would not say that we hurtle down the runway. We start to lift off at about 50 knots, which is about 60mph. Which is up to motorway speed in relation to your car, and it feels a bit like that at the start of take off. It is like accelerating down the slipway on to the motorway, until you take off. It can be quite bumpy on the grass strip where I fly, so we bounce a little bit along the runway on the take-off and then when we get into the air, I smoothly apply a little bit of back stick. I can feel the Tiger Moth wanting to fly, I can feel that moment. At the start, I do it by looking at the air speed, knowing that the air speed is going to take off about between 50 and 60 knots, smoothly apply back pressure and we go into the air. Now, I feel the aeroplane. I can feel when that aeroplane wants to fly. She is the same, she is saying, "Yes, okay, I gave you a bit of a hard time in the morning starting but okay, now we are going to do the business. Now we are going to go and I am going to show you what I am made of." The aeroplane's talking – not me.

My Thighs Have Control

As we take off, that is the moment that I love and I relax. It is strange: I have tried to figure out how to put it into words and it is quite difficult. I do not know whether it would be like sitting in a bath of warm chocolate or on a summer's day, paddling in a nice Mediterranean Sea or something like that.

For me – I do not know what other people feel, but for me – at that moment of taking off, I get a real sense of relaxing and I feel like I am coming home. It is that moment in the air when no phones can get at you, no e-mails; nobody can bother me now. I am captain of this aeroplane, I am in control, and I have the say so over what happens on this flight. I am in control of my own life, my own destiny; sometimes, I am in control of the aeroplane depending on how she is feeling. But I get that real feeling of elation and relaxation. It is very difficult to put into words, but that is one of the reasons why I fly. It is a real coming home for me and I just feel so at ease when we take off and I go, "That is it! I am in my domain." If you learn to fly or you fly yourself, maybe you will have the same kind of feeling.

The Tiger Moth is understood to be easy to fly but hard to fly well, and flying from an airfield where it is on a hill, you often get up draughts and downdraughts. So those are the first bits of turbulence that you will feel when you take off and you have got to fly through those and you have got to understand how to make it a smooth flight. I always try and make it a nice smooth flight for my customers because that relaxes them too. Sometimes you can hear them shouting that we have taken off however I give them a few minutes just to feel the whole 'open air cockpit, wind in your hair, real 1930s' experience, and it also gives me that little bit of time for myself – my flying and my aeroplane.

Then we head off to the local sites, castles, remains of Iron Age forts and lovely big houses, all of which are a phenomenal sight from a Tiger Moth: There are some sights that you can only see all of it from the air. It is a beautiful, fascinating way of showing people what you can actually see from the air. Then we start the fun. So, we are in the air by now and most of our customers for the Tiger Moth vintage flights are of the mature sort of stature – let us put it in polite terms – and quite a lot of them are slightly deaf. No, let's put this as a confession. Most of them are half-deaf and a lot of them are very deaf, which proves quite difficult in an aeroplane – in an open cockpit aeroplane with goggles and helmet that get used seven times a day by different people so therefore probably do not fit that particularly well and with an intercom that requires them to press a button to be able to speak to me and with all the wind rushing by. It is like talking on a motorbike, if you have ever talked on a motorbike. Or, next time you are on the motorway, safe and legal and there is plenty of room round you, wind down both the windows and try to have a conversation with the passenger, without looking at one another as well, and you will see that the wind noise goes up and you tend to miss things. Remember we are in tandem, so they cannot see what I am saying as well, which does degrade the amount that you can hear. I have no idea of the technical science of that, so do not ask me that one, but it does. I know that it does. If you are not looking at the person: a) you are not getting the body language; and b) you are getting a bit of the tone of voice but you are not understanding when the person's going to speak and what they are saying. So deafness does cause, I would say, the majority of problems.

Let me confess: here it is. They have taken their hearing aids out before they get in because they think that they will hear better without them. Mm. Yes, mm. I have no idea the thinking on that one and it is very funny what they will say. There must be lots of videos out there of me saying, "Oh, and here are is the Castle." And they will say, "Oh, is it really blue sky today?" And I will try again, "And on our right hand side you will see the Castle." "Good grief, can you see down to the Isle of Wight?" So, a lot of the time, I have to say, very slowly, very definitely, what I am trying to point out and I will also angle the aeroplane so that hopefully they will know that I am trying to point them to the left or right and show them what it is we are looking at. It it is quite funny the things that they will say and often they will answer back, "Blue skies," or, "Tuesday," to what I am trying to say. Then they wonder why I am laughing. If you think about it, it is a very weird thing that I do next. I then give them control of the aeroplane and let them try to kill me. So, for some of my jobs in life, I really do pay people to try to kill me. Let me explain on this.

I have control of the aeroplane and I am flying it from the back and we have briefed beforehand that I am going to give them control of the aeroplane so they can fly and see what it is like to fly a Tiger Moth. I have told them that very small movements give very big movements outside; it is like driving on a motorway, you only want to move it in millimetres, not in cm or inches. When we are on the ground, they see that I am doing big movements because it is like doing a three point turn in a car, however in the air it is like driving on a motorway. Of course, because we have taken off and it is an open air cockpit, that part of the brain has been left and blown away and is still waiting on the ground for them. So I explain all of that again and I hand them control and the first thing that most people do, even though I have briefed them that this is what they are going to do, is they get hold of the stick with a clenched fist, instead of just a finger or thumb, and the first thing they do is tense up on it. When you tense your body you bring your arm and therefore the stick back towards you, this points the nose up in the air and threatens to put us into a stall. Stalling, for the non-technical blondes, is when the aeroplane no longer has the upward lift it requires to keep itself in the air; it then falls in a very ungainly manner out of the sky and lands in a heap in the grass. So, stalling is a very bad thing when we do not want to do it and we are not in an aeroplane that we want to do it in, unless we are doing it on purpose. The first thing I have to do is put my hand behind the stick and stop them from grabbing it towards them. You would think it was something like an ejector seat or something, the way some people grab it and pull it towards them. I can eject them if they want: they could loosen their straps I could turn the plane upside down and throw them out, however they have got to pay me more money to do that.

By now they have been getting nicely relaxed only to get scared again by trying to fly, so I help them through a little bit and I say, "Look, here is how you fly. I am flying it with you at the moment; here is how you do it, with very small movements." Then they start to relax again and get the hang of: a) that I am behind them and I am actually going to save them; and b) it does take very small movements. I will say it again in big, capital letters; it takes SMALL movements to fly the aeroplane when it is in nice smooth air. Then they start to really enjoy it and say, "Yes, I can do this." And I shout through, "Are you having fun? Do you want to keep flying?" and they go, "You have control," and I go, "Oh, okay." So I try again and say, "Do you want to have another go at flying and are you enjoying it?" And they go, "Yes, you have control." So I say, "No, no. Would you like to keep flying it? Would you like to have another go?" "Yes, I want another go." "Okay, you have control." Then I know that they are not hearing me very well and just say nothing while they fly.

So then, to make it interesting for me, and because we have got this video strapped to the aeroplane, I tend to take my hands of the controls and I say, "I am just going to wave to the video to prove that you are flying." Then, I wave at the video, and depending on the time of year, I will wave for a long time or a short time. In the summer, I will wave for quite a long time and if they are flying it quite nicely and I am not feeling scared, at this point, that they are going to throw us upside down and bend the aeroplane and bend me, then I will possibly tell them to turn left or right and have a go at that. Just like you would on a bicycle, I stick my hand out left and right at the back, as they are turning to show on the video. If you have ever watched any of these videos, you will see me doing all kinds of little things. If they are in the front and wobbling about a bit, I tend to put my scared face on in the back, pretending that I am scared as well. I probably really should not do these kinds of things in the video because the CAA, the Civil Aviation Authority, will probably ring me up one day and say, "You are not in control of the aeroplane, are you?" Here is the secret though, and here is the confession bit that you must not tell anybody, this is just between me and you. When they are flying the aeroplane and I have got my hands out the cockpit and I am waving and pointing at them and doing an okay sign to the camera or waving that I am scared or turning right or left, what they do not realise is that ladies' thighs are slightly larger than the males' thighs and therefore I can actually reach the rudder pedals that control the tail/ rudder of the aeroplane and I can also gently cover the stick, the control column, so that they cannot do any massive movements that would turn us upside down or stall us. I am letting them fly however they have only a certain amount of play in it, because my thighs would stop them. I often wonder what would happen if I called through and said, "My thighs have control now." I think that would be entirely the wrong type of flight and entirely the wrong kind of message that I would be sending them. So, please do not tell anybody that I do that or else you will be in for the chop.

Also, the other great thing that most aeroplanes have is what we call a "trim wheel", which is attached to the elevator, which is the lateral flappy bit on the end of the tail that controls the up and down movement. As you flap the tail up and down, the nose goes up and down on the opposite end. It is like on a pivot as the air goes over it. So, basically, this trim is attached to the control stick by various wires and as you put the trim forward or back you can almost control the flappy bit on the end of the aeroplane, the elevator, within a certain range, without the customer knowing. I only allow the customers a certain range and they will find it very difficult to push and pull against the trim. So, I trim the aeroplane out to fly roughly straight level to keep us going nicely and I cover the control column with my thighs, and I have control of the power, of course, in the back. So, if they do anything that is really bad, I can either take off the power, depending on the manoeuvre that they do (for example, if they put us in a spin) or put the power on if they are trying to put their nose in the air and stall us. Again, this is our little secret, so do not tell everyone or else the magic will be lost.

Having said all that, they do fly. I really do let them fly it and again, this is going to sound completely wrong. You are going to take this the wrong way, however, the more comfortable they get with the aeroplane and the more relaxed they are, the more nicely they fly the aeroplane, the more I can let my thighs drift apart a little bit. I think we will leave it at that.

The View Out Of the Office Window

The other thing is, when we go up, it is normally either a 20 minute or half-hour flight, which means a quick tour of the local area. I give them a quick show of the local castles and the big houses and then give them control and then sadly, it is time to come back to the airfield. If we have an hour's trial lesson voucher, we can do things like go down to the seaside and go and see Glastonbury. It can be quite difficult to navigate in a Tiger Moth because once you get in; it is like riding a horse.

If you think about it, it is the same kind of area as riding a horse or sitting on a motorbike. So, if you can imagine you are sitting on your motorbike, or riding your horse and you have got to take one hand off to look at the map and hold the map so that it does not blow away in the 90mph wind because if you lift it just a little bit above the surround of the cockpit you will lose it, it will get taken by the wind, blown away and there goes your navigation. Well, at least you do not have to worry about your navigation because your map's gone and you can definitely know that you are lost because, again, your map's gone. It does cut out quite a lot of panicking about where you are because you just know that you are completely lost.

Also do not drop it on the floor of the aeroplane because, just like the horse or the motorbike, if you drop it on the floor, that is also null and void because you cannot reach down with the straps and it can slide underneath you, either in the front cockpit or down to the tail. So that is also a no-no. Also there is nowhere it can rest in the cockpit; there is no nice tea tray like on your airliner where you put your meal. You think it is bad enough in an airliner, where you cannot get your elbows out to cut your prime steak or whatever they are serving on the day? It is the same in the Tiger Moth; you cannot get your elbows out, so you cannot put the map anywhere. If you try and hold your map with your teeth, you have got your microphone in the way.

So it is quite a juggling act of where you put the map. I have got it sussed that I can either put my map just on the strap or slip it underneath the compass so that it can be in front of me, although most of the time I tend to just hold it with one hand and fly with the other. Or if the person in the front is flying and my thighs are quite happy, then I will hold the map and look out the window.

I will confess. I do take a hand-held GPS with me. Although, from what I have just described, it is equally as difficult to hold the hand-held GPS because the GPS has to see the satellites. So putting it on your lap is great; I have it on a big neck lanyard so that it does not fall out. I put it on my knee the first time I used it and it just kept saying to me, "No satellite reception. No satellite reception. No satellite reception." There are a lot of places in the world called, "No satellite reception." Yes, I know, that is an old joke. So the GPS needs to be held up to find the satellites.

Another well-known place in this country and abroad is "battery low, switching off". I have visited this place several times. I have found at least five of them in this country. So, your GPS switches off, and now you have got the problem of trying to get out the batteries because I am a good pilot I have actually taken extra batteries with me and they are in my leg pocket.

The first thing is, I have got to take my foot off the left rudder, which means the aeroplane will swing to the right first and then to the left and then the person in the front's going, "Oh, what is going on?" So I take my foot off, grovel around, get my batteries out and then try and change the batteries in the GPS without dropping them on the floor or throwing them out the window. This must be a very interesting video when I have to change the batteries.

However, the thing that most appeals to me about flying is the view out the office window. This is what I am telling the customer, now that they are flying it a bit and they have relaxed a bit, and they get to a point where they get tired. They have been flying it nicely in a straight line and we are navigating to where we want to go, we have looked over their house (they often want to fly over their house if they live in the area as well), so we have navigated there, we have flown over their house, and then they get a little bit tired and the aeroplane starts to wander. It is like when you are tired in a car and you start to wander, so I then say I have control and let them breathe a little bit.

Then, I get them to look out and say, "Look, this is the whole point of, or one of the biggest points of flying a Tiger Moth. It is the view out the office window. My view out the office window changes day by day, minute by minute, hour by hour and it is phenomenal and I love it.

This is my stock answer that, if you are reading this and you have flown with me, you will have heard this. I love this job and it is a great job for women. I get to boss men around all day: after all most of the customers are male. I get to look out the office window and nose around in people's back gardens.

I am amazed at how many swimming pools there are in this country. Why? Swimming pools in this country? Really? Are you sure? I have to say, this year, to date, I have not seen any of the covers come off the swimming pools. It is just a status thing? There are lots of tennis courts as well and there are some lovely, lovely houses, among which I have picked at least 10 in and around the area of the airfield where I am going to position over if I have an engine failure or anything goes wrong. Because I am going to land in the front garden or back garden, depending on where it is, and rock up to their door and say, "Can I put my engine fire out in your swimming pool please?"

I love it, and as I say, it is a great job for women. I get to boss men around, I get to nose in people's back gardens – it just needs to pay a little bit more and I would like to have the opportunity to wear different kinds of shoes and high heels.

Although high heels with these kind of aeroplanes do not go well together. Then it would be the perfect job – however I am working on that. When I tell the customers that, they have started to settle down and they are beginning to understand the intercom and they can normally hear that and understand it.

The Original Tiger Moth Pilots

Sometimes I am very privileged I get to take up some of the men that actually flew the Tiger Moth in the old days. I have never actually taken up any of the women. I would love to do that. I would be very privileged to do that, however I have taken up about five men that actually flew the Tiger Moths 70 odd years ago. They are in their 90s; they are normally very spritely, and they can get in and out of the aeroplane better than I can. They remember how to fly the aeroplane, although you do have to watch them because when you hand them control, they are remembering the days of their Tiger Moths, Spitfires and Harvard's and they are thinking, *Oh, I will just take this for a little ride.* Sometimes they might not have touched the controls of an aeroplane for 30 or 40 years. It is a privilege to fly with them – it really is – however you do have to be careful when handing over control because they sometimes forget for the first few moments what it is like to fly. Very soon though they settle down and you can tell after a few minutes that they have got back on their horses and they can fly very well.

I had an engineer who worked on the very aeroplane that we used to fly and he had worked on that very aeroplane, 70 odd years ago. It is fantastic when I meet these people because I ask them, "Is it true that you used to fly in a big round field, you used to point it into wind, you used to have lots of ground crew, and you used to train 7-10 hours on the Tiger Moth to learn to fly?" To which they say yes. In comparison, today, we train for 45 hours to get the first private pilot's licence. They would go from the Tiger Moth to the Harvard to the Spitfire in something short of 20, possibly 30, hours and how they did it, I have no idea. I have the highest esteem and I am very humble when I meet these people because of how they learned to fly: how they did it, how they managed to do it all and fight as well is unbelievable. That goes for the other side as well; there were young men and women on both sides however, it is a privilege to fly these people and the one man actually brought his log books up and it was amazing. He had pictures of all the different Tiger Moths he had flown and we went through all of them. He had not flown the particular one that we were flying however he had flown, something like 15 different Tiger

Moths and 7 different Spitfires. I turned green with envy just looking through his log book. It was such a privilege to read his log book unfortunately I did not have enough time to pour over his log books because we had the next customer waiting, but it was fantastic.

Occasionally you get these people and they are very humble normally. Yes, they will talk about flying during the war if you ask them however they do not offer it up first. Normally their families say, "Oh, he learnt on Tiger Moths." The veterans themselves are humble about it and they just want to enjoy the experience. Again, some will look at me sometimes and say "Oh, you are a woman pilot," however they are often very used to it because a lot of women flew the Tiger Moths when they were flying. So they are quite happy with it. Normally they come back from the flight with the biggest Tiger Moth smiles on their faces because it reminds them of all they have done. They will probably never fly a Tiger Moth again and it hopefully brings their flying full circle. There is never enough time to talk to these very interesting people.

Taming The Tiger Moth

Windy days give the Tiger Moth problems, when you cannot fly because of the cross-wind in relation to the runway. The aeroplane itself has a cross-wind limit of 10 knots; we work in knots because a lot of aviation terms and practices come from sailing. Which means if the wind is blowing across the runway at 15-20mph, the aeroplane itself will not be able to handle the take-off and landing because it runs out of what we call aileron authority which is the flappy bits on the wings that make it turn from left to right. And when you are coming into land, those are the surfaces combined with the rudder that keep it heading straight on the runway. Wind is one of the biggest problems and explaining why to people that it is not safe to fly. Because if the wind picked up the underside of the wing, the bottom one, the plane would cartwheel over and we would end up in a heap and that would not do me or the aeroplane or the customer any good. But trying to explain that to people who are familiar with modern airliners that have cross limits of up to 35 knots, which can be up to 45mph, is quite difficult because again they have got this conception in their mind of what an aeroplane does and how it does it and it is like a vintage car. You would not put a vintage car into a Formula One race.

Another bit of fun of Tiger Moth flying and why I love doing it and the challenge of it is the take-off and landings. The take-offs are pretty much: if you put power on and hurtle or smoothly go down the runway, you will take off. But the landing – that is a whole different kettle of fish. During the landings – and this will make sense to people that fly – on the video, you will see the customers come down and as I touch down for the first time they will say, "Oh, that was very smooth," but then we bounce and take off into the air again, and they are just finishing their sentence off, "That was a very smooth landing," as we bounce for the second time and then on the "-ing" part of the "land-," we will probably come down for the third time. By the way for the technical people I am talking about very small bounces here not a rebound into the air. This is what levels the playing field across the whole board: if you cannot land the aeroplane, you cannot fly. It is as simple as that and no amount of money, prestige, character, ego, nothing, will save you. If you cannot land that aeroplane, you will end up in a heap on the floor.

That is what I love about it because in all walks of life you have to be able to do the basic, you have to land the Tiger Moth, this aeroplane will laugh at you when you are coming in to land. You come in to land, you have got it all set up nicely, you are in the right place, the right height at the right speed coming down smoothly and the wind will just kick the Tiger Moth a little bit and she will go, "Yes , I am going to have fun with you today on landing." She picks up the wing and you catch it and you put it down the other side and you overdo it a little bit so you start this sort of seesawing sideways as you are coming into land and the Tiger Moth's just sitting there, going, "Yes, I am going to bounce you all the way down the runway and laugh in your face," and she does. She does that. She just comes down and goes, "Yes , that will be one landing, yes , two landing, three landing," and then you think, "Oh, this is terrible," put the power on, and go around. I have had days where I have felt the Tiger Moth is literally laughing at me and I come down and I have to apply the power and do what we call a go around – which is putting the power on and taking off again and going all the way round and coming back down – because you know you are just going to bounce it all the way down. If you have too big a bounce, you can damage the aeroplane and yourself. It is very funny because I really feel that the aeroplane is laughing at me as I fly my approach and landing.

This is the challenge of flying the Tiger: the landings are always different, always new, and if you sit and watch tail dragger landings, you can always learn something. Woe betide somebody who turns around and says, "Oh, that was a rubbish landing in a tail dragger." You never hear that. You never hear somebody come out and tell you seriously that you had a bad landing however you often have the joke that you will have to pay three landing fees for your three landings. So, on some days, the landings are smooth and on some days the landings are bouncy and what will happen all depends on how the aeroplane is feeling and how she is either wanting to make fun of me or not. No, I jest: it is all experience and it is all technique and I can feel the other tail dragger pilots laughing at me now. If they were truthful they would say their aeroplane laughs at them too.

The Naked Pilot

Now, I want you to picture the scene: the dashing World War Two Spitfire pilots walking out to their aircraft, each in an immaculate uniform with not an oil stain to been seen, the sheepskin jacket slung over the shoulder with ease and the white silk scarf gentle blowing behind, again with not a mark on it. The uniform was made to fit a male form and accentuate it. Now that you have the romantic picture in your head, here comes the reality.

When flying, I do like to look nice. I know I am not a fashion icon; however, just looking nice would be good. Maybe one of the things that put women off flying is the stuff that you have to wear. Certainly, when I wear the stuff for the Tiger Moth, you can understand why. Okay, so they used to wear nice silk scarves and I thought, *Hey! That would be cool!* Yes, until it tried to strangle me whilst flapping about in the 90mph wind! I do not know how they did it. I think they used to have them dangling down nicely for the photographs, but then in the air you need this thing wrapped round your neck tightly and stuffed down inside your jacket so that it does not flap around in the 80 mph wind and strangle you or try and wrap itself around the aeroplane and kill you because it is gotten wrapped around one of the control surfaces. So, that is the myth of the scarf gone then, for the fashion police. I do have a scarf with nice little Tiger paw prints on it and I have got a white scarf, however I tend to use a ski neck warmer, which is a round piece of material that fits nice and close to your neck to keep you warm and has no flapping bits left out to cause any problems.

The sheepskin jacket I do wear, though, because it is very warm and very durable, as there can be small sharp bits of wire that catch less resistant fabric. Even recently I have had to patch up my sheepskin jacket; however, the fashion police might actually approve of this as it has that 'lived-in' look now. You can have either the leather ones or the sheepskin jackets, depending on your fashion statement, and I have two: one for the winter time and one for the summer time. My summer jacket was actually real fashion, bought in a high street shop as aviation coats are now back in fashion, as is a lot of the 1930s clothing. I am very pleased about this one. I bought it discounted, £10, in the sales after Christmas and thought, *That will be perfect for my summer Tiger Moth coat,* and it is. Which is really nice because in the summer I can break away and wear just a little bit less clothing.

I am not talking about the naked pilot here. No, no, no! I have never ever thought that being naked and Tiger Moths go together. Far too cold! I have flown naked though. Quite a liberating experience as no one can see you really, so you feel really naughty however you are not being outrageous. For those who are going to go in for naked flying, here is a tip. If you get undressed before getting in the aeroplane then put your clothes somewhere away from the slipstream. As the running around after finding my clothes was not so exciting, enough said I think.

The Fashion Police

For vintage aeroplanes, you normally wear a baby grow, or people call them 'grow bags', because for some people, when they put them on, parts of their anatomy grows. I am talking about their heads and their egos. What were you thinking? They are actually technically called a flight suit. You know the type: the one that the Red Arrows wear and the one that all the military pilots wear that you step into with both legs, then you struggle into it, looking most ungainly, over your shoulders and then breathe in while you realise you should not have eaten that extra cake as you zip up the front. It has a nice little zip at the bottom of the torso that you can unzip if you are feeling that you need a bit of air down there. Apparently, the bottom zip is something – for men! And yes, going to the toilet is a real pain in the shoulders as you struggle out of it, desperate for the loo, with the zip doing a battle for its life not wanting to unzip now, and the top half of you doing some kind of ludicrous dance as you shrug off the top part of your flight suit.

Once you have struggled into your flight suit/grow bag, it is actually very useful and actually normally made out of quite hard-wearing stuff. It takes the oil and the fuel that tends to get splashed around on you, and tends to soak it up quite well and does not stain that much. Also, when you are climbing in and out of these aeroplanes, there are lots of tiny little bits of metal locking wire – not sharp bits of metal – just sharp ended wire that can tear less robust clothing. Jeans are not always the perfect thing to wear just by themselves. I wear a pair of jeans underneath my flight gear.

To complete the exercise of getting into the flight suit, there are then zips at the bottom of the suit to enclose your legs in case ferrets try to get up your trouser leg. Then the arms are also protected by either zips or Velcro straps to encase your wrists. It brings to mind a picture of S&M, with all this strapping and zipping. However, by the time you have sweated – or glowed, as ladies do – and struggled like an escapologist into this contraption, I am sorry to say that any thoughts of romance or bondage have disappeared and I am more worried about the ferrets.

Even in summer, I have jeans, some kind of tee-shirt or polo shirt, and then the flight suit and then the jacket on top. Maybe that is because I am a 'cold fish' – quite a few of my ex-boyfriends have told me that, so it must be true! I have heard rumours that some people do not wear anything under their flight suits. How romantic! Well, maybe; however, remember that sweating is normally what accompanies flying in this kind of aeroplane when you are on the ground and these flight suits maybe say hello to a washing machine once in a season. Mine, of course, has a positive affair with the washing machine, or at least twice a season. Once, right at the beginning of my Tiger Moth flying, someone offered me a flight suit to wear to keep warm and I declined politely, thinking the flight suit did not need the Tiger Moth to fly – the fumes alone coming off the suit that got used by everyone could have filled a hot air balloon and the suit could have gone flying by itself.

To further assault the fashion police, you then have different electric hats you can wear. Some people wear what we call 'bone domes', which are like motorcycle headwear. I have to say that is the perfect one for safety. However, I found it a bit unsafe for me personally because every time I stuck my head outside the cockpit to try and take off and land; the weight of this 'bone dome' in the actual air stream would flick my neck back quite a lot. Therefore, I found it very uncomfortable and very difficult to fly well in a 'bone dome', which is why I use the leather hat instead. It is a personal choice deciding which you want – and purely for the 'fashion police', I tend to think that the leather one looks better. I am trying to get a fully leather one because, in the old photographs, what you see is that the pilots just had a leather helmet, they did not have to have an 'electric hat' as my instructor used to call it. Head phones were not required and they do stick out rather a lot and make you look a bit like a teddy bear gone wrong. When aviators first started flying biplanes, they used just to have these nice leather helmets that maybe had a furry lining. They would slip them on and look so glamorous with their little silk scarf dangling down. These days, the big head phones that stick out at whatever angle, just do not seem to be glamorous at all.

You then have the goggles. If you put them on and have never worn goggles for motorcycling – just goggles, not visors on helmets – you will know that I say: you cannot see very well at all. This, of course, is what I blame my bad landings on. It is a real art trying to see and look out of these goggles; however, you do have to have something that protects your eyes because you are travelling, as I say, between 70-100 mph in the air. Basically, if a bee, wasp, or even a small fly hits your goggles, you need some good protection because you do not want that going straight in your eye.

To finish off the ensemble, I wear a nice pair of gloves. I tend to wear two pairs of gloves. I cheat! I have a nice, very thin pair of silk gloves, which feel lovely next to the skin. Remember that you have had the hand cream of the oil and the avgas on your hands before drying them out. Then you slip your hands into these silk gloves and they feel lovely. I then wear the standard white leather military gloves on top, which these days are looking a little bit oil-stained and a little bit grubby. I probably need to invest in a new pair, although it goes to say that if you have a brand spanking new pair of white gloves, you obviously have not actually flown or even looked at a Tiger Moth, because as soon as you look at the Tiger Moth you get covered in all kinds of oil and fuel and bits of grubby stuff that you do not want to even think about. It brings a whole new meaning to 'playing dirty'! It is not the nice kind, unless you are into that sort of thing. I do like the smell of aviation fuel; however, from afar. It tends to rot your hands if you have too much.

So, the white gloves go on top and that keeps my hands warm enough. If your hands get cold, it is very difficult to fly the aeroplane. The aeroplane laughs at you again. If your hands are cold when you are trying to come in to land, the aeroplane's going, "Yes, told you so! I told you your hands would get cold!" In the winter, I have the nice silk gloves, of course, and then I put a pair of big thermal gloves over the top: ski gloves again. Skiing has improved the lives of vintage flyers fantastically. I did try skiing; however being attached to the ground all the time was a problem because I kept taking off, and not when I was supposed to. The landings were terrible and very undignified, but I have put a lot of my ski gear to good use over the years.

What has happened, I wonder, to the 'fashion conscious pilots' these days – in the olden days, I think they perhaps looked a little bit better; however, they were maybe colder when flying. Now we are slightly warmer because we have got all our thermal gear on however, I tend not to look quite as dashing as the olden time aviators used to.

A Bank Robber Pilot

One of the expectations I have found when around vintage aircraft is that people expect you to look the part. People expect you to wear some of the vintage gear when they are being offered the trial flight vouchers. They want to wear the gear as well and they are happy to dress up in the leather jacket. We give them a leather jacket and the helmet and the gloves and so on. I tell them, when they are stepping out there, "You have to look as silly as I do, or else I am going to feel left out!"

A magical day was when Rita came over and said, "We might have a difficult customer because he is just over there." I turned to look and this man had turned up and was dressed head to foot in original flying gear with the white silk scarf, the leather jacket, even the sheepskin boots and it was all hand-stitched and perfectly authenticated. I thought, *Oh!* You know when you turn up somewhere and you are a bit over-dressed and you think, *Yes, I read the invitation wrong.* It was like that and I was a little bit unsure about this. I was scared; never mind about him, so I bounded over to him and said, "You are my next customer," and he came back with, "You are a woman." We both looked at one another and I was thinking, *You are worried about me being a woman when you are dressed like that?* "Who's more weird?" was the more appropriate question.

Actually, he turned out to be a really nice man. I was a little bit worried when I said, "Oh, I am very glad that you have come dressed for the occasion. I expect all my guests to make such an effort." I said, "Is uniforms one of your hobbies?" His partner said, "Oh yes, you should see the collection he has got at home." It sort of hung in the air at the end of that question. I was thinking, *Where do I go from that? Do I say yes, no?* "Am I really sure I want to know about your uniforms at home?" I asked. He laughed and looked at me and said, "I have got a warehouse full of 200 costumes." He makes the uniforms for films. That is his job.

He had just finished making the costumes for the James Bond films, as well with the military ones. He has made a lot of them and he was such a fascinating person to talk to and when I asked about him wearing this one, he said, "Well, I had got this uniform in the back and I thought, *Why not? Why not dress up for the part and come and do the whole flying thing in the authentic uniform?*" He was more authentic than the aeroplane.

So that was great. He was one of our very special customers and I really enjoyed flying with him too. A good day for fashion, I would like you to take note, if you are reading this and are going to come up and fly with me. I expect a certain amount of dress code from my customers from now on.

However, if we are getting onto the confessional front here, I bet you would love to see what I wear in the winter. In fact, if you are of a delicate disposition, you had better not read the next bit. It would destroy your image of the 'sexy' pilot, if there is an image of the 'sexy' pilot. For winter, I tend to wear two pairs of walking socks. Walking socks are fabulous – they have got these thermal heat-radiator things in them and they are brilliant. Add to this, thermal long johns; thermal vest, tee-shirt, a fleece, then my big sheepskin jacket, two pairs of the gloves – the silk and the thermal pairs – and then, to top it all off, just in case my customers weren't scared enough that they are flying with a woman pilot, they then have me putting on my black balaclava headgear. In the winter time, I find my face and my head get really, really cold – and my neck – so I found a lightweight balaclava that was actually for micro-lighting purposes. I put this on and it comes down and literally gives me just a little slit for the eyes, so you get the full bank-robbing effect. When I walk out and the customers are taking the pictures and they see me in my bank-robber balaclava, it is no wonder they are a little bit scared! They are actually going to go flying with me.

A Micro-light aircraft and a vintage aeroplane actually hold a lot in common. Some of them are both open to the wind; open cockpits – some of the more fixed wing micro-lights have closed cockpits but they are still quite cold. They do not have a heater in them, so the clothing that we wear is actually quite similar. Flexi wing micro-light pilots tend to wear big padded baby grows – big padded flight suits that do actually look more like baby grows, big cuddly teddy bears really. They have similar wind limitations, from when they can take off and fly, and also the same difficulty in juggling maps and charts in the air. You will see that most pilots of the flexi wing micro-lights have their charts hung round their necks on piece of strings, in plastic folders, so that they cannot get wet. It must be difficult for them to write anything on the charts as they are flying along. Just like in the Tiger Moth, it is difficult to write things on the chart whilst flying.

The reason I am calling them 'charts' and not 'maps' – we will just have a little bit of science here; a technical tip for blonds – is they are called charts because it is something to do with cones and circles and topographical stuff. Do not ask me! I passed that exam; I passed it first time actually, the navigation exam, thank you very much! Think of a chart as a working document that shows what has changed on the surface that you are flying over, which is one of the reasons we need new ones each year. In contrast, a 'map' is more of a reference book telling you a representation of what is on the ground. Basically, we need a 'chart' to plot navigation with, as that is the one that shows us the most relevant details for flying. Again, I am not trying in any way to make this a technical reference book more a general flavour for flying. If I refer to the charts as a map, you will probably understand what I am talking about. You can breathe now the lesson is over, although there will be a test later.

The clothes you have to wear for commercial flying are equally as terrible re: the 'fashion police' stuff because basically all of the flying gear that is designed: the flight suits; the coats; the boots; everything like that is all designed for men and so are the uniforms: the black trousers; the white shirt; black tie; all of that is designed – probably by men – to look good on men. Therefore, it does not look particularly good on women. When I get dressed up in my commercial gear: the black trousers; the white shirt and black tie, I look a bit of a cross between a sad lookalike for the Blues Brothers and an overgrown school girl (not the sexy kind either), rather than having this very fashion-conscious commercial pilot look. With the black tie and the black trousers, if I put the balaclava on from the Tiger Moth gear, I would be a dead cert for a bank robber.

One of my boyfriends also used to say that I did not look very attractive in my pilot uniform, especially when I put my tie and my bars on – my shoulder bars; the gold brocades that you put on: either two bars or four bars depending on how big your ego is for the day. However I looked, if he was not interested in making me feel good when I was wearing my uniform, then I thought, "Hmm! Maybe I should get a new boyfriend!" And that is just what I did.

Pilot For Hire Anyone?

A lot of the time when I turn up for the commercial jobs, I get the same thing. "Oh, you are a woman. Or is it you flying? Or oh, are you not the hostie? Oh!" Grrr. If I hear it one more time, I am sure I will take the fire extinguisher to somebody. I do understand, though; I really do. I am a lady pilot and most people have this image of commercial flying that, when they turn up, they are going to be faced with a jet: sparkling; freshly washed; red carpet treatment. They are driven through the airport, where they have hired their personal aeroplane with their personal pilot. They hire it through a broker and do not really understand what they are getting most of the time. The broker puts a very small picture at the bottom of the email to show what your aeroplane is and what it looks like. The normal assumption is they think they are going to be picked up by their limousine; driven through the gates of the airfield, bypassing all security; all passport checks; all government checks; driven straight up to the aeroplane, where the red carpet will be; the sun will be glinting off the jet and their glamorous hostie will open the door for them; they will climb the stairs to their jet to be greeted by the pilot who is very good looking; a little bit more mature; a little bit of silver in the hair; who says, "Please sit down. Enjoy your champagne and read the newspapers. The flight will be perfect. The weather is perfect. The hostess is perfect. The pilots are perfect. The aeroplane is perfect. Everything is perfect. We will arrive early and it all will be perfect."

There is my bit of fiction writing. Now I will give you the real version! I turn up (a lady pilot) in the Ford Fiesta of the aeroplane world, and the look on their face is priceless! They have not been driven to the airport in a limousine. Yes, they have been stuck in the charter side of the airport but they still have to go through security and passport checks. I will paint you the picture of the bargain basement end of charter flying.

It is quite a small aeroplane, the kind of little aeroplanes that people learn to fly in; stick two engines on it at the front with little propellers on the front. That is the first thing. They are thinking, *Why has it got wind-up toys at the front and has not got a jet engine at the back?* There are no steps to get into this aeroplane. I just give you a knees-up and throw you in. You cannot stand up in this aeroplane. You have to squeeze yourself down into it and we have to squeeze your ego in afterwards. There may be a tray table, but if you can

Confessions of a Lady Pilot

get the tray table out and to work, then please do not because we can never get it back in again. The catering will be handed to you in a little freezer bag with lukewarm coffee, and various stages of squashed sandwiches. There will be no champagne on this flight because if you open a bottle, you will hurt the aeroplane and the champagne itself will fly everywhere because we are operating with the same pressure inside and out of the aeroplane; i.e. an unpressurised aeroplane. So, the fizzy drinks all want to get out of the bottle very, very quickly when you open them. The customer is now in the aeroplane and depending on which bargain basement aeroplane it is, I have either to climb through the cabin pass them to get to the front cockpit or I have to leap up onto the wing, very dextrous and cat like, and climb in the front.

So I can understand why the customers are a little bit scared again. However, I have only had one refusal. She was a lady who was very, very scared of flying anyway. To say she had a 'silver spoon in her mouth' would be putting it politely. Her husband had hired the aeroplane, although for a laugh he had not hired a jet, and I was taking her abroad to meet him. At the start, she flatly refused because: (a) I was a woman; and (b) there was no toilet on the aeroplane. I do not know which was worse: the hassle of the customer or being put in the same category as a toilet! However, I explained everything that was going on. I phoned my company and there were no jets available. There were no jets from the airport. I did do my best and eventually she got into the aeroplane. Actually, at the end of it, when I brought her back (we went over there and came back), it was one of the very few occasions on a commercial trip where I got a tip, so she must have been fine at the end of it.

I can understand the look of horror on the faces of customers also because the reality of the glamour of flying in charter jets or charter aeroplanes is not red carpets; it is smelly carpets because the aeroplane has been stored overnight and there is a little bit of mould that you just cannot find in the carpets. It always smells a bit mouldy. The catering leaves something to the imagination. It is not champagne; it is lukewarm water or possibly lukewarm orange juice if your company really splashes out. For the pilot, it is bargain basement hotels or bed and breakfast places that are miles away from the airport. Normally, even the taxi driver does not even know where this hotel is. The only bit of blue sky on the weather that you are going to see when you start charter flying is the tiny little bit on the artificial horizon, which is one of the instruments that is on the instrument panel in front of you and half of it is blue and half of it is black. As long as you can see the blue bit, then that is the blue sky you will be looking at.

This is the reality of it. You will end up smelling of oil and avgas again because you are checking your aeroplane out and they have a habit of leaking and chucking fluids at you because the aeroplanes themselves like to sit and laugh at you. The aeroplanes themselves are maintained to a standard – kind of. However do you know what my favourite customer to fly in the charter world is? It is not people; it is not freight. It is dogs!

Now, I know you are going to look at me really strangely. I love flying dogs – not the flying dogs of your imagination, the flying dogs that sit inside. The dogs that can afford to charter an aeroplane for themselves; normally silver-spoons-in-their-mouths dogs. Sometimes the owners come with them to annoy me. However, the first class dogs I have found are very well-trained. You walk them out to the aeroplane. They will cock their leg, normally against the aeroplane, which is a little bit irritating, but hey, at least it is not inside the aeroplane! They know they are supposed to go the toilet before they get in. You give them a quick drink of water. You get them in.

They come with their own rug, which is fantastic. You spread the rug out on the seats; they sit on the seats; attach their lead to the safety harness; sometimes they will even come with their own little safety harness. You strap them in. They do not require catering, as they normally bring their own. Dog Chocolate drops actually taste quite nice (it was a long flight and I had forgotten my sandwiches). They do not require entertainment. They do not require being told what the weather is like. They do not require being told the time to the destination. In fact, they do not want any conversation at all because they want to look out of the window, just like you. Or even, best of all, they get in knowing it is a journey and go to sleep.

The secret to flying dogs and making them come back and fly with you again is to slowly climb up to your destination height, and to fly smoothly and around the weather (which is true of people as well) so you do not make it too bumpy for them. Then, when you are descending at the other end, make it a nice shallow descent of about 700 ft per minute, which is half as shallow as an airline descent. As you cannot turn round to them and say, "Here is a mint. Suck a mint" on the descent, or on the climb-out, so it hurts their ears if you descend or climb too high or too fast. Then you will have a very unhappy dog, which will whine, or worst get sacred and then you have to clean the aeroplane.

As long as you know that tip, the dogs will be fine because dogs that travel in charter aeroplanes are very well trained and they may not be a pedigree variety but they know their place and what they are supposed to do, and they are used to doing this. They are used to getting into some kind of vehicle and being taken to somewhere where it is going to be nice, so they know what the score is.

You are normally given their bowls, so you can give them a few bits to eat. They do not normally need a drink in flight unless it is really long; however, they always want a drink at the end of the flight. Take them out, give them some water, and give them a few of their titbits. Again, they will cock their legs on your aeroplane, which is still a bit irritating but you have got some water; you can wash that off, and that is it. Luggage is minimal for dogs. Fantastic! No problems with the weight and balance. There is always, always somebody to pick them up. I have never ever had somebody late to pick up 'darling little Pickles'. Even if it is not the owner, then the dog still gets picked up in a nice car or Land Rover. If you are taking them abroad, they have always got their passport. They do not need to do a security check. The passport's done and that is it. You are away! It does help that I love dogs however, the best customers to fly in charters, from my thinking, are personal pet dogs.

Anyone Can Do It If I Can

Why did I want to be a commercial pilot? Well, I never thought I would have the chance. When I was a kid, I always hoped that I would be a commercial pilot, but with time, money (lack off) and men, (getting in the way) it just did not seem possible. When I started my commercial flight training, I ended up being the only woman again. Very few women train to be pilots; however, as I was growing up I thought it was completely normal to follow my dad in whatever he liked. My dad loves aeroplanes and loves remote-control model aeroplanes. He never had the chance to become a commercial pilot; however, he has always been involved in the remote control model world. He himself is quite a 'mover and a shaker' in the flying water plane model world now. He made a replica of the Water Hen, which if you imagine the Wright brothers' aeroplane and put floats on it you have the idea. It was the first float aeroplane to fly in this country on Lake Windermere. My dad is my inspiration to fly.

So I was brought up picking up broken bits of model aeroplanes for my dad in fields at weekends when I was a kid: me and my brother. I just thought it was quite normal. I was not into dolls. I was into aeroplanes. I made a little Red Arrow and hung it above my bed. My brother wanted to be a fighter pilot, so when we were on holiday, my mum and dad thought it would be a good idea for him to go and have a flight in an aeroplane to see if he actually could stand it and to see if he really wanted to do it.

We could only afford the 10-minute flight. At a beautiful airfield called Enstone, in the Cotswold countryside. My brother had a flight in a motor glider and I was the annoying little sister who said, "Well, if he is having one, I want one too!" So I was given a quick 10-minute flight as well. My brother went up; came down again and said, "Yes, I am still going to be a fighter pilot. It is fine," as teenage boys do in that kind of tone of voice. "Yeah, whatever. Nothing impresses me." I went up and we left the tarmac and went into the air. I do not remember anything of what this man said to me, this instructor. I was just looking out of the window thinking, *This is the most amazing thing I have ever done. The view out of the window is just amazing!* I had a real affinity for looking down at the ground and thinking,

Wow! – Towns and fields, and where we were – and I loved it. I had that feeling of being at home in the air. I suddenly realised: *This is part of what I want to do in my life. How on earth am I going to do it?* Up till then I was going to be a dancer.

It was amazing, just that feeling of freedom; that you could do what you wanted when you were in the sky. The aeroplane would turn and go round in circles and do what you wanted. It seemed so easy to me. It seemed, you went left – if you wanted to go left, you took the stick left; if you wanted to go to the right, you took the stick to the right; if you want to go down, push it forward; if you want to come up you pull it towards you. It felt really normal; it felt really at home.

I have never lost that feeling of freedom and elation and of being at home in the air. When we landed, I got out and I had got the motor glider grin on my face. My mum took one look at me and went, "Oh no!" That was the start of it, really.

However, I lived in a place up near the Lake District where there are not a lot of airfields, so I had to learn to drive before I could fly; I had to get a job before I could learn to drive. As I had left school at the age of fifteen, with no worthwhile exams. I walked out and got a job. We went for a gliding holiday, me and my dad, when I was quite young. It was fantastic! I did a loop in a glider and also got to fly above the clouds. When you fly for the first time ever in a small aeroplane above the clouds, it is magical. You feel you can reach out and touch these things. On the top of the clouds, when you have got the sunlight looking down on the clouds, they are white and fluffy and you could walk out and skip along these clouds. You could touch them. It is the most amazing feeling in the world.

Nobody can hurt you up here; nothing can get to you. There are no phones; there is nothing to do apart from fly and feel free. All you have to do is be in harmony with the aeroplane that you are flying and make it do whatever you want it to do and hopefully the aeroplane will be behaving that day, so it will do what you want it to do. It is just that magical feeling of freedom, of pure concentrating on what you are doing. I loved it!

So, after a bit of wasted time, enough money and after a few men got in the way, I finally got to start my flight training for my PPL. I trained at an airfield called Tatenhill, which is an absolutely beautiful place to train and has fantastic instructors. I went up there and said, "Teach me to fly in that," pointing at a tail dragger, which is an aeroplane which sits with its tail on the ground and its nose in the air. The instructor said, "No. That will be too expensive. I will teach you on this first," pointing at the Cessna, which is a high wing tricycle undercarriage aeroplane.

I said again, "Teach me in that," pointing at the tail dragger. He said, "No, I am going to teach you in that first." This went on for a bit. I eventually said, "Oh, okay then." So he started teaching me in the Cessna. We had fantastic fun, amazing fun! It is that old joke of, "How much fun can you have with your clothes on?" Flying, for me, was just that. It was just amazing, and words never really can convey how I feel about it. How good it makes me feel and how relaxed I am when in the air.

Achieving The Im-'Possible' Dreams

The day I went solo was the day that changed my life. Everybody who flies will tell you about their first solo. I was so surprised because I had apparently been ready for it months and months before and then the aeroplane had gone tech, the weather had gone tech and I was not available. It is a standard happening when you are coming up to taking your solo, or even your test. The day I did it, the instructor went, "Right. I am bored. I am getting out now." He got out of the aeroplane and I took off and the aeroplane climbed and shot into the sky because you have less weight. Then you are taking off and are going around the first corner before you know it. Then, when you settle down, you do not really realise that you are flying by yourself. It is only when you relax a bit into that first flight by yourself – when your what is called 'downwind', which is running parallel towards the airfield going in the direction of the wind and you are starting all your pre-landing checks – that there is a moment where you have a little bit of time to yourself.

I was going to say something and looked across to where the instructor should have been sitting and he was not there. I realised this was it! My life was completely in my hands. If I lived or died, it was completely up to me. Whatever happened, nobody could influence me; nobody could save me; and nobody could do anything about it. Yes, you hear on the films that people can be talked down. Well, where I soloed, you are talking about an airfield where, if they turn the radio on in the morning it was good, let alone be able to talk you down.

So there was no talk-down. There I was, flying this aeroplane for real, bearing in mind this is a person, this is me, who has been written off as a kid in school and been written off in so many jobs and been written off in so many other fields of life. All I would be good for is stacking shelves, I remember one teacher saying to me. There I was, floating in this aeroplane: me being trusted with this aeroplane and flying all by myself. It was such an empowering feeling of, "Wow! Is this really happening to me? Unbelievable!" I suddenly realised that, yes I could and would land this aeroplane and that maybe just maybe I could achieve anything I wanted if I put my mind to it! Maybe the impossible dreams would turn into the possible dreams?

All too soon, you are late downwind and turning towards the runway getting on with the business of flying, you have to start doing your pre-landing checks. Then you are working hard on final approach and throughout the landing, as you know no one is there to save you. I came in to land and as I touched down – and it was quite a nice touch down – I rolled in. I was speechless! As you can imagine, that does not happen a lot with me.

I was on the verge of tears. I did not know what to do with myself. I wanted to jump for joy. There was so much adrenalin in my body; so much exhilaration in my body; so much realisation of what an achievement I had made. I was useless! I was actually doing my degree at the time and had a presentation to do in a couple of days' time. I had so much adrenalin in my body, which I now understand, that I did not actually sleep really well for two nights and I made a complete hash and failed the presentation I was doing. All I could think of was, "I want to keep flying now. I have flown an aeroplane by myself. I really have. I can do anything now because I have flown an aeroplane." I must have been the most boring person to talk to because I relived the whole 10 minute flight in glorious detail to anyone who would listen and told strangers in shops that I could fly an aeroplane. It really is a life changing moment. Try it.

That is why I try to encourage anyone and especially women to have a go at flying. I am not saying I do not encourage men as well; however, flying an aeroplane is a real empowerment thing to do and it is just such a fantastic moment of achievement. Whatever else you do in your life, for that one moment you have flown an aeroplane and landed it safely, and landed it well, and you have been in complete control of your life. It is not like driving a car. You can get out of a car any time you like. Even on a motorway, you can pull up to the side and get out, but when flying an aeroplane, there is only you that can get it back on the ground.

That is the biggest kick and now, as an instructor, it has gone full circle. When I send people solo, I still get that 'high', because they get out and they have got that look on their face of, "Do I cry? Do I laugh? What do I do? I am speechless! I want to hug everybody." It is that real euphoria and I get that as well now. Ask any pilot about the first solo, they will still remember it.

I carried on and learned to fly and, as soon as I got my licence, my Private Pilot's Licence, I said to the instructor,

"Teach me in that! The tail dragger," and this time he did. I got introduced to lots and lots of adventures during my PPL years: air racing, which is a whole other story. That was where I got introduced to flying the Tiger Moth. I had already picked the Tiger Moth as an aeroplane that I wanted to fly. One of the things you can do when you have got your Private Pilot's Licence is to fly to France for lunch, which is so cool. When you go back into the office Monday morning and the usual question is, "What did you do over the weekend?" some replies are "I went to the pictures." "I decorated the toilet." "I mowed the grass." "What did you do, Amanda?" "Oh I just flew to France, me, piloted my own aircraft; flew to France; took passengers; we had lunch and I flew back." There is nothing like it! This is where the ego starts to get a little bit big, you see. I felt like finding everyone who had ever written me off and said that I would never achieve anything. Telling them I could fly them to France for lunch because I am capable, safe and legal pilot, however I won't fly them to France because they wrote me off to be a loser. Well, who is the loser now?

What A Weird Way To Make A Living; People Trying To Kill You Every Day

Time, money and men got in the way again and I had lots and lots of fun doing lots of exciting things, including air racing in the Schneider, in which I won the women's race – again, that is a whole other story – doing the Dawn to Dusk twice, which is a competition awarded for the most enterprising aviation – again another story and another book.

Circumstances in my working life then gave me the opportunity to think that I could become a commercial Pilot. So I bit the bullet and did it. Again, you have to remember that this is the person who stepped out of school at 15 with, I think, three GCSEs that were worthwhile. I had eight GCSEs all told, but only three of them that were any good for anything. I went on to pass all the commercial exams through grit and hard work and I had something that my mum used to call 'seven o'clock in the evening'. I used to ring her at seven o'clock in the evening, almost in tears, saying, "I will never do this. Why have I done this? I will need to go back to my old job – I will have to find another job. I just cannot do it." She would say, "Yes, it is seven o'clock in the evening." I would say, "What are you talking about, mum?" She would say, "Yes. It is seven o'clock in the evening. I think you have been studying all day. I think you should close your books, have a bit of tea and watch the television; and wake up tomorrow morning and it will all be okay."

I realised that she was right. Yes, mother you were right, on that subject at least. Actually again a huge thank you to my mum without her support I would never have achieved anything in my life. After a long day's studying, including writing this book, you do: you get to the seven o'clock in the evening where your brain is just 'fried'. My very good friend who then took his commercial ground school used to ring me up with the same worry as me, and I used to say, "It is seven o'clock in the evening." When you get to seven o'clock in the evening, close whatever you are doing and start again the next day. Believe me, if I can do it, anybody can do it.

I passed my commercial piloting exams just as the recession hit, which was really bad timing because I had decided to go commercial because airlines were just sucking people up. As soon as you walked out with your Commercial Pilot's Licence, people were being sucked up straight into the airlines so I was almost guaranteed a job. That sentence in itself is a stupid thing today. Nobody is ever guaranteed anything. So there I was: no job. What to do next?

Well, I knew I wanted to teach people to fly and possibly do aerobatics in Tiger Moths. So I started down the road of flight instructor and what a weird way to make a living is being a flight instructor! You basically get into a small Ford Fiesta of an aeroplane and allow people to try and kill you on a daily basis. For five hours a day, these people are doing their utmost to try to kill you. No not in the axe murderer way, I will explain. You get in with this student. They are sitting next to the keys. One of the things that students like to do, when they are going through their checks, is to turn the keys off, which stops the aeroplane and you are kind of like, "Hmm. That is a little bit inconvenient because we are about 50 miles away from the airfield!"

When you are coming in to land and you have got things called the flaps down, which is basically putting the brakes on in the air, they will take them all off again, which makes your aeroplane sink, which means you come down towards the ground at an awful fast rate of knots in the wrong direction.

You are there with your bottom cheeks clenched, hoping that will save you from hitting the ground, having done a go around, which means abort the landing and apply power and go around for another try. Your hand is pushed as far against the power as you can push it as you will the aeroplane – this Ford Fiesta – to try and get back into the air.

Because, of course, these planes are 30-odd years old, so it takes them a little time, and they have to have their laughing moment. They sit there and laugh at you and go, "Yes, you did not watch this student well enough, did you! Well, I will just get as close to the ground as possible before letting the power do the work and launch into the air again."

Students do all kinds of funny things. If you are flying in a low wing, they have fuel tanks in each wing and you have to change the tanks every half-hour. The button to change the tanks is also the button to switch the fuel off. Students can manage to switch the fuel off in flight, which again proves interesting when you are 50 miles away from the airfield and you have forgotten to bring your handbag, so therefore you have forgotten to bring your diversion bag and mobile phone.

I learned very quickly in both the commercial world and in the PPL world to take a bigger version of my handbag, which contained a little overnight kit containing my toothbrush; a spare pair of knickers, make-up and some deodorant. "Why," you ask me, "is deodorant involved in flying aeroplanes?" Well, if you come and fly aeroplanes you will understand! When people are learning to fly (me included), the brain seems to tell the body to overheat and sweat, thinking that will help the situation, which it doesn't, of course. It just makes me very thankful for deodorant and wishing that other people would use a little more of it.

So it was a very weird job that I ended up doing, "Yes. I really do let these people try and kill me!" You are teaching people to learn how to land. One of the most complicated things to do and instructing means after demo-ing a landing for them, I am trying, just with my mouth, flapping my lips, trying to instil into them how to land. They cannot see me; you are sitting side-by-side or tandem seating – trying to tell them how to land this aeroplane without killing me or bending the aeroplane.

I tell you, it is a real art. It is really funny sometimes, the stuff that students do. Freezing is another common axe murderer trick. I think they are doing fine and then they come down to about 50 ft above the ground and they will literally freeze on the controls and they are quite strong, these people, sometimes. I have to try to wrestle them off and say, "I have control," whilst their brain just literally explodes. The saying is that the brain has a moment where it breaks wind inside itself and just freezes for a moment and the person can do nothing. People in this state just sit there and freeze. It is in slow motion to them however I have to grapple the aeroplane off them, fight it off them and go round again. Then I cannot turn round and shout at them, "What are you doing? Why are you trying to kill me?" I have to turn round and, in a nice voice, say, "Well, so we have learned from that landing that we do not freeze as we come down on the controls, and if we think we are making a bad landing, we do a – what we call 'go-around'. You apply the power and go around – *sooner* this time please before you freeze on the controls!"

All The Gear And No Idea

After a while, I got promoted and taught on what they call 'glass cockpit' aeroplanes, which sounds funny because you think, "Well, apart from the Tiger Moth, which even does have a little bit of a windscreen, surely all aeroplanes have a glass cockpit because they have glass on the outside do not they?" There are some really funny statements in aviation.

'Following through' is another thing you have to do when you are an instructor, which sounds terrible when you first say it. "Follow me through," – basically means placing your hands and your feet on the controls in front of you when you have dual controls and following what the instructor is doing through their controls so you get the motor skills through actually looking and also feeling what the instructor is doing.

Going back to glass cockpits, it is basically not the surround that is outside you; it is the actual instruments in front. Normally, in old aeroplanes, you have got instruments that have all this magic stuff in them called little gyroscopes. Technical tips for blonds: gyroscopes are basically like a spinning top. They used to say like a kid's spinning tops. I never had a spinning top. Did you have a spinning top as a kid? So no wonder we do not know what these gyro things are. Basically, if you think like a spinning top or if you get a bicycle wheel and hold it by the skewers, and get somebody else to turn the bicycle wheel really, really fast; then try and turn with the bicycle wheel, you will feel an opposite, conflicting direction in your body. That is a basic gyroscope.

This is what the old instruments are made of, and pressure instruments and air and all kinds of magic stuff inside them. Now what they have done in the airliners, and also it is starting to come a lot into smaller aeroplanes, is the 'glass cockpit', where you have a computer screen, normally two computer screens in front of you, that show you what the old-fashioned dials used to show you. They are phenomenal! I am a bit of a strange pilot because I love vintage aeroplanes and I also love the new modern stuff. The stuff that is in the airliners, where you can dial up what your number four engine's doing; you can dial up and see what number 135 passenger is doing and why they have been in that toilet for so long with the number 287 passenger – no, I am kidding! That is what the hostie is there for: to police the naughty behaviour.

These glass cockpits are amazing. They have engine management pages, which are phenomenal; fuel pages, and when flying in instrument conditions, which is basically flying in cloud, they have full maps. However, they are rubbish in, rubbish out. They are a computer. If you put rubbish in, you will get rubbish out.

Interestingly enough, these aeroplanes normally cost a bit more money and therefore you tend to get people that have perhaps more money than sense. Notice I said "perhaps". There are an awful lot of good pilots out there. I am just trying to give you the best confessional bits. There are very, very good pilots that fly these aeroplanes however the worst one I ever encountered was somebody who would not do any flight planning; or any technical planning; I have no idea how he got his licence. He got his licence abroad somewhere and came over to this country to try and fly these aeroplanes in this country, where we have a lot of controlled air space that you have to understand. You have to talk on the radio and if you have all this state of the art kit, then why not use it? He basically did not want to do all the home work for it. I find it strange that the same kind of man will get a new mobile phone and spend hours playing/learning how to use the latest gadget on the phone, but when it comes to the aeroplane – forget any learning. They expect to just jump in and press buttons and the aeroplane will magically read his mind, produce a flight plan, fly and divert round the weather because it has looked at the weather, touch down on landing with the lightest touch, and then park itself and refuel, ready for its next flight. Oh, is that all my job as the flight instructor? I seemed to have misread the job description again!

I remember one day turning around as we were coming in to land – and I thought this was going to be a rubbish landing again – and I just said, "Pass me your wallet." He said, "I beg your pardon?" He was actually listening to me, which was good. I repeated, "Pass me your wallet, because hopefully with the amount of money in there, I will chuck it underneath the nose and that will cushion the landing. That will save us because that is what you are doing with your flying. You are just chucking money at it and you are not actually learning how to fly." The strange thing was that, after being a little upset at me, he always wanted to fly with me after that. I am not sure the feeling was mutual.

So, you do get some interesting people. Funnily enough, my first job in the commercial side of things was ferrying bank stuff, not actual money by the way. And before you ask it would not have been enough money to disappear with and live a life of luxury anyway, you would need a bigger aeroplane for that. I was ferrying freight. This was flying at night over the Irish Sea in rubbish weather. I always used to think this was a weird job too because, without going into too much detail because of the security side of things, let me just say that stuff is transported all round the world and when it gets picked up at the other end, the people that pick it up are… well… not what I expected either. I must have given them a 'look' as they gave me 'the look' of, "Oh, you are a woman pilot." I looked at them and went, "Oh, you are here to pick up the bank stuff?" Believe me; they looked like the bank robbers! Again, they actually turned out to be really nice people, doing a job that most of us would hate and for not very much pay.

There were some good moments and some bad moments in that job. It is very high workload, flying at night in cloud over sea all by yourself, which is called single pilot operations. Not that the aeroplane knows that it is over a sea, but you do and your backside knows that you are over a sea. I thought it was quite ironic, actually. My first commercial job as a pilot was flying bank stuff, and my first job when I left school at the age of 15 was working for a bank. I had to re-sit my English as part of my employment contract.

Funnily enough, I never fitted into that job because people used to say to me at the age of 15 or 16, "Ah, you will love working for this bank because you get a cheap mortgage." I would reply, "I am 15-16. I want to fly around the world and be a pilot. I do not want to think about a mortgage." Those were the days.

Tail Dragger Pilots Make The Best Lovers

Well, the first thing is you have to drop your ego when you fly Tiger Moths because not only are the landings humble makers, but the fact is, you cannot actually stuff your ego into the aeroplane and then squeeze the doors shut. This is because the problem is, in an open air cockpit aeroplane as the Tiger Moth is, your ego is seated nicely around you as you are taxiing out, however as soon as you open that throttle and start down the runway and begin to pick up a bit of speed, your ego is blown severely off and scattered all over the runway behind you.

So you cannot have an ego and the aeroplane lets you know that all the time. It will laugh at you if you try and fly with an ego, and that is why I love it, actually. I love flying open air cockpits because also, for the men, you have to leave your ego behind. It really does; it makes you humble and the Tiger Moth is possibly one of the hardest aeroplanes to land. It requires perseverance and it requires being able to laugh at yourself and knowing that the aeroplane will spend a lot of time laughing at you as well, and as long as you understand that, you will get on great.

I often think I should take my whip out and give the aeroplane a few lashes before I get in, to teach her to obey me first, however that is a whole other story and dangerous territory. I have heard that pilots make the best lovers; have you heard that? When you get into the niche of it, I have heard that tail draggers, as the Tiger Moth is a tail dragger, make better lovers or the best lovers of all.

Well, maybe, and yes, I have to say there are a few pilots that are good lovers however let me ask you this, again this is between me and you in confessional mode: I started to think about this and I thought if they are such good lovers, how did they learn to be such good lovers? Maybe they had lots of instructors and lots of teachers and I was sitting there the one day thinking, *Hmm, maybe I am not the only aeroplane that this person flies...*

True to form, I went out with one pilot and we went out for dinner, all very nice and romantic, and I sat there and I said, "So, how come you are not married? You are good looking, you are a pilot, you are a good catch, how come you are not married?" He said, "Well, I just didn't... decided not to." He lied, basically. Blatantly lied. Fortunately, I ended up not inviting him in for coffee and, a few weeks later, I again met this pilot. He had been a bit strange and I thought things were a bit strange. He was at an air show, wandering around, and I was going to bound over to him and say, "You have not rung ..." Although it is not strange in itself that men do not call me, but I bounded over to him and he was a bit standoffish and I said, "Hi, everything okay?" He replied, "Yes, absolutely. Here is my wife, Victoria." "And here is my daughter." The penny dropped, "Ah!" I said. I so missed a money opportunity making there, did not I? I could have said to him, "Well, that is going to cost you, isn't it? That is going to cost you three meals that you are never going to eat."

However I have been thinking, now that I have been flying Tiger Moths for a while. Maybe the Tiger Moth itself, the aeroplane, is the best lover. The aeroplane herself takes a while to get into the mood; you have to have quite a lot of foreplay to get this aeroplane started, push her out of the hangar, get the oil lubrication moving around her. It takes her quite a while to get into the zone and when you take off you get that exhilaration, you get the feeling that this is going to be really good and, as you are climbing up into the sky with full power, the whole aeroplane vibrates around you and through you and you have this control column, which is a big stick in front of you which sits in-between your thighs and it vibrates when you have got full power on. So maybe the aeroplane itself should be characterised as the best lover and maybe that is one of the reasons, if I confess fully, why I like flying Tiger Moths. Apparently you get the same kind of feelings from riding a horse and because this book is in a different kind of genre, I think we had better leave it there. I will be writing those kind of books under a pseudonym, or else I will never be able to fly again, will I?

So, these days, forget the pilots; go for the aeroplane. They make the best lovers. I agree. Tail draggers make the best lovers and it is true: how much fun can you have with your clothes on? That is a very old saying.

Well, believe me; there are not many days in an open air cockpit in the English countryside where you would want to fly the Tiger with no clothes on. Believe me, there is nothing sexual about that bit at all. It is freezing on most days. I tell the customers and the passengers that I fly with, "When you have got your coat, your flight suit, your scarf, your hat and your gloves, if you are a little bit uncomfortably warm on the ground, then you are possibly going to be at the right temperature when you get in the air." I have never heard anybody who said they were too hot when they flew in a Tiger Moth.

Now, I am sure that somebody out there is going, "Well, I am too hot." However, in my experience, I can never get warm enough. I sometimes feel okay and do not feel too cold however, for me it is definitely the most fun that you have with your clothes on.

The other thing that goes back to the lover thing is that the vintage aeroplane world seems to attract more male pilots than it does women pilots. Now, I would love to find the reason for this and I try to encourage women, ladies, to come and fly these vintage aeroplanes. They are extremely good fun.

It is fantastic challenging flying and it will make you a better pilot and it empowers you to be a better person as well, and yes, there are so many men and so little time, as the one lady said. However, the problem is a lot of the male Tiger Moth pilots are in the slightly mature range, I have to say, which is fine, because we get checked every year as pilots for our heart conditions, there are not too many 80 year old millionaires with dickey hearts with no encumbrances on their wills that are flying the Tigers.

I am sure there are dashing Spitfire pilots that come to mind, like the pilots in the Battle of Britain, the film where you see them all, looking amazing. I have nothing against men, but there does tend to be two types of male pilots, the happily married type of pilot and then the pilot that has a girl in every port… airport. I do love men by the way, and love being surrounded by them most of the time. So don't tell them that my number one lover is the Tiger Moth, just keep that to yourself.

Falling In Love With The Tiger Moth

But why would you want to fly a Tiger? Well, even before the first flight that I ever took in a Tiger Moth, I had looked at these aeroplanes and fallen in love with them, the whole look of them. They are beautifully made; they are beautifully drawn. The man who designed them, Geoffrey de Havilland, was a moth collector, an entomologist, and he drew the aeroplanes as he saw the moth, which is why they are all called Leopard Moth, Puss Moth, Tiger Moth, etc. They are all named after real moths and he drew the aeroplane based them. She looks beautiful with lovely curves. We are going back to the sexual connotations, however she is a lovely, lovely looking aeroplane and she is beautiful. It was this iconic aeroplane that I fell in love with and I thought, *I have to fly that aeroplane. I have to fly that aeroplane some day and I have to fly it commercially someday*. This thought went through my mind when I first saw this aeroplane and I thought, *Yes, do not be daft*. As usual, I have been told, like many of you, "Do not be daft. Put that thought straight out of your head. Move on."

When I went air racing, there was a man who had a Tiger Moth. The person whom I had flown down with knew that I was obsessed with Tiger Moths and he went and asked the Tiger Moth pilot if I could fly. I was wearing a skirt because it was one of the nice summer days and I was not thinking that I had the chance to fly. I was so shocked when the man came over and said, "Would you like to fly it?" He was one of the more mature gentlemen, a lovely, lovely man, and I thought, *Hmm, how am I going to get in this with a skirt?* Well, I need not have worried because there were an awful lot of people that gave me a lot of hands to help me climb into this Tiger Moth, which is like getting on a horse really. If you think of getting on a horse in a skirt and not riding it side-saddle, then you get the picture. Fortunately, I do always have the best underwear on. My mother taught me well: Always have your best underwear on because you never know what is going to happen in the day. Therefore, everything was fine.

We took off and we were flying round and he gave me control of this aeroplane for only a few minutes and I fell in love right there and then and I thought, *This is it! I have to be able to master this aeroplane one day!* I had not even gone solo in any aeroplane by that point. I had only just started on my private pilot's licence.

Many years later I achieved yet another impossible dream and started to tame the Tiger Moth. Time, money and men always get in the way of your flying – or time, money and women, depending on which variety you wish to go for. The Tiger Club, which is down in Kent is the home of the Tiger Moth and they have G-ACDC, which is one of the oldest registered aeroplane in this country. She is beautiful; she is in a maroon and silver colour and I fell in love all over again with this aeroplane and thought, *This is it! I have got to learn to fly this aeroplane.*

The first thing they say to you is, "Well, we will start you in a Cub," which is a different aeroplane. I said, "No, I want to fly the Tiger Moth."

They said, "Yes, yes, yes," pat on the head, nice little girl, "You start in this aeroplane."

"No, but I want to fly in that one."

"No, you start with this one."

"Okay, fair enough. I will start with that one." *Where had I heard that before?* I thought.

Anyway I started with the Cub and moved onto G-ACDC. Then time, money and men got in the way of my flying again, so I had to leave the Tiger Club for a while. I will be back.

While I was flying from the Tiger Club I was taken up in ACDC with a person who has become a good friend and he showed me a cloverleaf aerobatic manoeuvre in a Tiger Moth and again I thought, *I have got to do this. I have got to be able to learn to do this one day.* So, thank you for that, and thank you to the people that gave me my first experiences in Tiger Moths. I truly have never forgotten those flights. They will stay with me, tattooed on my heart forever.

A few years later, I had the opportunity to start learning, to actually start my Tiger Moth training for real; I could not wait. *Excellent.* Get my teeth into it eventually. I started learning at Cambridge, where they have the most spotless Tigers ever. You could eat your dinner off these Tiger Moths. They gleam; they are polished, and they are polished, and they are polished, and then they are polished some more and then they fly and then they are polished and they are polished again. Cambridge is good fun and they are one of the only places that actually train for your private pilot's licence right from scratch on a Tiger Moth.

Again, things got in the way – time, money and men – and I ended up at a place called Sywell, where I was given an instructor whom I shall call Mr Grumpy. However, Mr Grumpy, for all his outward grumpiness, is one of the kindest, nicest, best instructors that I have flown with and he was the person who eventually set me solo with the immortal words of, "I am bored with you now. I am getting out," which is quite common amongst instructors, and I thought, *Where have I heard that before?* I was sent off to solo in this Tiger Moth by myself and as I was taxiing out, having soloed before in various other aeroplanes, I knew that this was the moment out of all those years that I was accomplishing a dream. One of my dreams was coming true – and remember, you are talking about a girl who was written off at school, who left school at the age of fifteen with a couple of GCSEs, not enough to get a job or to go to college – however I have now failed and passed and failed and passed and failed and passed my commercial exams. An Honours degree and a commercial pilot's licence later, there I am, sitting in this aeroplane that I have been in love with for years, wanting to fly this thing and I have made up my mind to fly this aeroplane. It was probably about ten years previously that I had first seen this aeroplane and thought, *That is the one I want to fly. That is one of the aeroplanes that I want to fly. That is on my 'must do' list of life.*

From those very humble beginnings after that solo flight, I now get paid to fly in the aeroplane that I love. That first solo flight in the Tiger Moth I have to say, when I got to do it, taking off it climbed better in the air without the weight of the instructor in the front, and I was told just to go and have a little bit of a flight and then to do three landings. I went off and had my own little flight and I was so tempted to point the aeroplane towards France and just head off into the blue skies. It was one of those magical moments where you feel really in tune with the aeroplane, with the beauty of this aeroplane. She was behaving herself; I was behaving myself. It was all going well. It was just one of those lifetime moments that gets tattooed on your heart and you just know that whatever happens, this experience will stay with you for the rest of your life. Thank you Mr Grumpy for the best training in the Tiger Moth.

After the landing, I came down and, even though I say it myself, the landing was very nice. I went and did three landings, which were all very good and then, I have to say, on the last landing I was thinking, "I do not want to come down," and the aeroplane was the same. The aeroplane did not want to come down as well, but I taxied in, and packed the aeroplane away – you wipe her down with an oily rag – and we went into the bar afterwards. I was standing at the bar and all these pilots are talking crash stories as usual, and I could feel a little tear coming in my eye and I thought, *That is it! I really have accomplished an impossible dream that I never thought would come true and I never thought I would be able to be here becoming part of this tail dragging society and of these old mature men* … sorry, mature men… *who take for granted stepping in these aeroplanes and flying them*. I was brought very quickly down to earth by the instructor saying, "You are not crying, are you? Is there something wrong?" How do you explain to somebody like that? I tried to explain to them and for five seconds, I think, they remembered their solo, then they moved on.

I then flew the tamed Tiger some more and landed at sunset, which was one of the most beautiful experiences of my life. Flying around in sunset with the aeroplane gives you the best pictures, of course. And still my thoughts where, *wow, this is me; this is really me flying this. This is the girl that is been written off so many times and yet here I am, flying this aeroplane and being trusted with this very iconic vintage aeroplane to fly it.*

I was then rung up by a caller who asked, "You fly Tigers, don't you?"

I answered, "Yes, absolutely."

"Would you like to come down and fly Tigers for me?"

"I would love to."

So I was checked out by the instructor to make sure I was okay and I said, "Well I have not got that many hours in a Tiger Moth."

He said, "No, that is fine. We will go and fly," and we went and flew and came down and there was a little bit of crosswind. He said, "How are you feeling?"

I said, "Yes, I think I am okay."

"Excellent, here is your first customer."

No pressure then.

Of course, the first customer was an hour's flight and they wanted to go down to the seaside and I had not really sussed the whole map reading thing while having a customer in front in the Tiger Moth. So, it was all a bit of a surprise to me to go down to the sea. Fortunately, it was a nice clear day so I could navigate quite happily down to the seaside and back again, however that poor customer never knew that I was learning how to navigate around a new airfield. When I was on that flight, I felt little bit like the ATA girls, who were given the aeroplanes, "So there is your aeroplane, just take it, off you go and fly it from Bournemouth to Kent," and it is kind of like, "Okay."

In my small little voice I went, "Okay, that is fine, I will do it. I am sure I will."

You know that you are capable of doing it; you have been trained to do it however the little gremlin that sits on your shoulder goes, "Yes, you think you can navigate in this aeroplane?" However, I did, and I beat the gremlin. I felt like a little bit of an explorer that day and, as they say in the good books, it all ended happily.

One of the best things that you can say while in the Tiger is, of course, "Chocks away," at the beginning of the flight before you taxi. So when you come down and watch me flying, you will see me waving at the ground crew Al and motioning for him to take the chocks away. Please feel free to shout along with me "Chocks Away!"

Why Do We Fly? Icarus, Freedom, Empowerment, View, Challenge, To Feel Like An Explorer All Of The Above

So it was quite funny that after all those years I was again doing a bank job. —My mum often says it is very weird because she has got two children that are very weird. My brother did not go on to be a fighter pilot. He went on to work in the engineering side of things – not aviation. He also went on to dive. His passion is diving and he is a very competent diver and has done all the diving things. He has his own version of the baby grow. He has this big padded diving suit. It is very nice, actually. It sparkles. It is got all these little sparkly things on it, which I am sure the fish appreciate. I am sure the fish must rank the divers out of ten for their fashion sense. "I like his suit. His suit sparkles a little bit," I can imagine the fish saying. When my brother reads this, he will kill me! It is lovely and one day he did the whole thing of actually dressing up in the diving suit so we could take a picture of him, like in the film: Mrs Robinson, where he wanders out in the whole diving gear. All joking aside, he is a very competent diver and is a dive master.

My mum said it is very weird. She has two children who are just not happy being on the ground. They are weird. My brother likes to be under the sea and I like to be in the air. She says, "What did I do? Where did I go wrong? Why are these children not happy at just being on the ground?" What makes us do these things? What makes my brother dive? He does cold water diving and dives with the oxygen and the tanks, all the compressed stuff that to me is horrifying. He dives in the dark, in cold water. I could not think of anything worse, however then again he might think that flying in an open-air cockpit in the middle of December when the snow's on the ground is equally as stupid. Why would you want to do it?

So why do pilots want to fly? Well, Icarus was the first person that tried to fly. Maybe it is that whole 'freedom' thing of getting in the air and actually being free and being able to do what you want to do with the aeroplane. I know it is the empowerment side of things. It does my confidence good and I have seen it in my students. It does their confidence good and the number of people who fly and improve their confidence is fantastic.

I love the view out of the window too. The view out of the window is spectacular at all times. Okay, a couple of times in the night-time when it was cloudy from the moment I took off to the moment I landed were a bit disorientating with me thinking, "I am not sure that was a flight," however the nights when it was clear and I could see the stars, and shooting stars was unbelievable.

Of course, when I am doing the exciting things like the Dawn to Dusk challenges, I feel a little bit like an explorer and I want to go on and do more things like that. I know this is not for everybody; however I would hope that everybody would experience a flight in their lifetime and experience the pleasure of flying. I know that there are instructors with varying degrees of competence out there that will give you different kinds of flight, but a good instructor should take you up, give you a safe trial lesson flight and give you something to really look back on.

Egypt is the furthest I have ferried a small aeroplane from with my friend, Mark. That was a very exciting explorer trip to do, over quite a big expanse of water called the Mediterranean. That is another whole different story. He is quite an inspirational pilot himself and I am sure you will be hearing more of him as well.

The Schneider was the pure need for speed. You have heard the saying, 'the need for speed' and please do not say you have not heard of the film. I know I am getting on a bit but I am not that old! I have only competed once. I have flown in a lot of air races as navigator but I only competed once. The 75th Anniversary of the Schneider Air Race was the one I competed in. I won the ladies' race there. I know there were only two of us ladies competing in it; however we had a bit of a 'thing' going about who would win. My fish was bigger than hers in the end! There is that ego again.

All those adventures – the Schneider, the Dawn to Dusk and Egypt – are something that I will keep for another book, if you are not too bored and I have not put you to sleep yet.

The Real Glamour Of Flying

Lesson 3 in the Private Pilot's Licence is the 'Air Experience Flight', getting accustomed to the aeroplane: a trial flight. Basically all it involves is taking you up and seeing: (a) if you are comfortable in the actual surrounds of the small, sometimes cramped cockpit, aeroplane; and (b) if you actually like the sensation of flying and if you have any kind of affinity with it. The view out of the window always makes it interesting and when people say they want to fly over their houses – that always makes it quite interesting for me because I have to navigate to their house. You would be amazed that they will show me where their house is on the map beforehand. I will navigate to their house, I will get to the village, town, road, wherever it is they say; I will point it down and say, "Well, that is where you told me your house was." You would be astonished at the number of people who have not got a clue where they are and they say, "No, that is not my house," and they will only spot it when you have circled twice. They will spot it half way around the second orbit because that will be the way they drive up to their house.

What I have figured out is that we can have all these satellite, internet maps we can look at; however, the actual getting in an aeroplane and flying and looking at the ground is a very, very different experience. It always amazes me the sort of disorientation of people when you first get up there; however, do not let that put you off. It only happens once and as soon as you figure it out, then it makes sense, and a lot of people can navigate back to the airfield if I start to point out clues to them. I think quite a lot of people are put off by the fact that they have to use a map. Yes, you have to use maps to get through your exam and yes, you have to use maps if you navigate, however if you want to be a commercial airline pilot, the maps and charts that you are going to be using are basically motorways in the sky. The airline charts are paper maps and have straight lines drawn on them. They have not got topography i.e. they do not show you what is underneath. They are just literally straight lines: motorways in the sky.

It is 'horses for courses', where flying is concerned. One of the most wonderful things after a trial flight in the Tiger

Moth was the customer who had been a little bit scared, he was a 92-year-old man and we got him in and he had done the whole looking at me, I am a woman pilot thing. When we got down from the flight and we landed, he said over the intercom, "That is the best thing I have ever done in my life."

I thought, *Wow! I should have kept that video for legal and boasting purposes!* I could not believe it and he got out and he was telling everybody that. I thought, *That is actually the biggest compliment that I could ever have, thank you. Somebody said that was the best thing. Me, humbly flying them around and just showing them a little bit of my world and landing fairly okay was the best thing that he had ever done.*

It took me a while afterwards to think, *If that was the best thing he had ever done, I wonder what the rest of his life was like?* As one of the slightly more uncouth men at the airfield pointed out, "What was his sex life like, if that was the best thing he had ever done?"

I won't go there! I took it as a compliment and I will leave it as a compliment, thank you.

I want you to have a go. It really is easier than you think. It takes perseverance and effort. That is what it takes. You do not have to be the brainiest person. I am not the brainiest person; I am not the most co-ordinated person. I fail a lot of the written exams and have to re-take them. Therefore, it really does take perseverance if you want to do it. I am the proof: If I can do it, anyone can do it.

Honestly, the empowerment that you get from somebody saying, "That was the best thing," scrapes away all the stuff about them turning round and going, "Oh, you are a woman pilot." It makes it null and void when they get out at the end of the flight with a Tiger grin on their faces.

Of course when we have landed and got out of the aeroplane all thoughts of me being a 'women pilot' have been left in the clouds in the sky and I have just become a Tiger Moth pilot. The first thing the customer wants to do is shake my hand and sometimes give me a kiss. Lovely, however again if you have ridden a motorbike you will know that the wind in your face makes you nose run. So the real art of flying is how to discreetly wipe your nose on your hand and then shake hands with the other hand, so the poor customer does not get covered in snot. They also have a runny nose so I have to try and not get covered in snot when being kissed by grateful customers when they have enjoyed their flight. Welcome to the true glamour of Tiger Moth flying.

Never Fitted In Until Now
My Home Is In The Sky

I feel that I have never fitted in, at school or in various jobs – and there have been a few. I felt I have never fitted in with any of those areas of life and now I finally fit in. I feel really comfortable with flying; I feel really comfortable with the people; I feel really comfortable with the aeroplanes. I feel that I have come home. I really feel that the sky is my home and I relax when I am up there. It is really, really good fun. Of course, at the end of the day – at the end of a good day of flying – you will find all the pilots in the bar, having a drink and talking crash stories.

This is something you take with a pinch of salt. After a few beers, too long into the night, pilots will start talking about the time when they flew through a thunderstorm and were only saved from the hail by bare inches; the landings when they have bounced all the way down the runway and have only just barely scraped in; the cloud flying they have done when they have only just scraped through the cloud and come out the other side and been able to survive. It is almost worse than fishermen. The fish get bigger and bigger. I am sure if there was a prize for the biggest crash story that pilots have survived, you would have people catching the equivalent of blue whales in aviation.

I try not to talk about my own 'crash stories', but of course I have had my fair few. No crashes for real, you understand, just situations that could have turned into a crash. I know this is "Confessions of a Lady Pilot", however if I start to tell you my exaggerated crash stories, the Civil Aviation Authority (police of the skies) might have a word with me, so I will leave those to the imagination. If you look very carefully throughout the book, you will see the true confessions anyway; however, I always make it safe and legal; safe and legal flying for the first reason: that will save your life and second save your licence!

So, always go out and fly safely and legally and have fun with it. There are huge amounts of fun to be had in this aviation. The people are fantastic, even in a world dominated by men. Especially in the vintage world – it is all about the challenge of flying the aeroplane every day. It makes you into a real sort of family with a real 'can do' attitude. There are an awful lot of people who go up there and 'do' fantastic flying and do not brag about it. There are amazing people out there and there are amazing stories.

So, go down to your local airfield and start getting involved. If I can do it, anybody can do it.

Watch this space! I will be working on bigger and better vintage and Tiger Moth flying, and I hope to see you all soon, with the blue skies and happy landings!

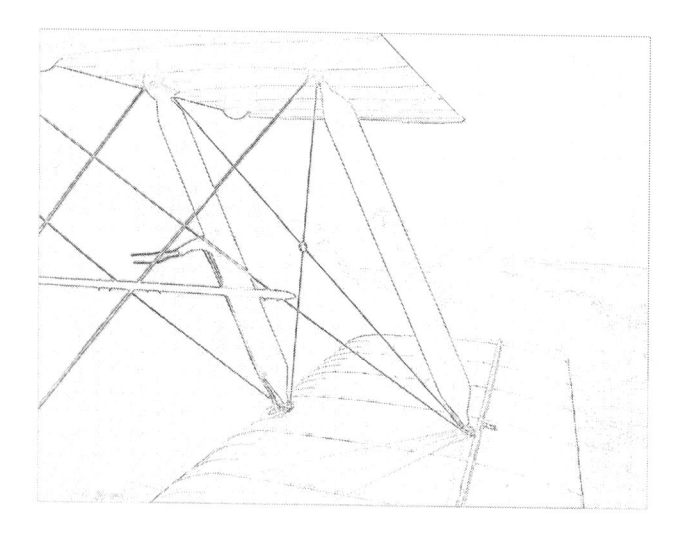

Made in the USA
Charleston, SC
01 September 2015